Sippy Cups Are Not for Chardonnay

Sippy Cups Are Not for Chardonnay

and OTHER THINGS I HAD TO LEARN AS A NEW MOM

by Stefanie Wilder-Taylor

SIMON SPOTLIGHT ENTERTAINMENT

New York London Toronto Sydney

SIMON SPOTLIGHT ENTERTAINMENT

An imprint of Simon & Schuster

1230 Avenue of the Americas, New York, New York 10020

SIMON SPOTLIGHT ENTERTAINMENT and related logo are trademarks of Simon & Schuster, Inc.

Manufactured in the United States of America

First Edition   13 15 17 19 20 18 16 14 12

———————————————————————————————————————

Library of Congress Cataloging-in-Publication Data

Wilder-Taylor, Stefanie.

Sippy cups are not for chardonnay : and other things I had to learn as a new mom / by Stefanie Wilder-Taylor.—1st ed.

p. cm.

ISBN-13: 978-1-4169-1506-5

ISBN-10: 1-4169-1506-0

1. Motherhood—Humor. 2. Mothers—Humor. 3. Parent and infant—Humor. 4. Mothers—Life skills guides. I. Title.

HQ759.W5 2006

306.874'3—dc22

2005035100

———————————————————————————————————————

❖

Typography by Ali Smith

For Jon and Elby—for turning me into a family

ACKNOWLEDGMENTS

First of all, there isn't enough Ketel One on the rocks with tons of lemon juice to thank my hilarious, supportive friend Chelsea Handler for believing that my edgy thoughts on parenthood needed to be published and trying to make that happen. Thanks to my agent, Michael Broussard, for making it happen. Yes, I believe you! As a first time author, I lucked out to have an incredibly insightful, patient, and funny editor, Patrick Price. Thank you to the rest of the team at Simon Spotlight Entertainment—especially Jennifer Bergstrom for being warm, gutsy, and innovative, and for taking a chance on me.

I would also like to acknowledge my old "mom" friends, Cynthia Sobo, Kristin Clark, Heidi Lipka, and especially Carolyn Darling, who came out of the woodwork when I had a baby, to offer love and support and humor despite the fact that I hadn't spoken to a few of them in let's just say a very long time. I get it now!

Also my new mom friends Julie Jordan and Lara Tochner—thanks for making me feel less like a freak in the world of motherhood.

To my friend Lisa Sundstedt, heeeeello, thanks for always being someone I can count on and for listening to lots of boring baby shit.

Thanks also to Cecily Knobler for constantly saying

"you can do this"; Dr. Peter Shulman for being an extraordinary pediatrician (he practices in Encino, California); and to my babysitter and friend Andrea Ward—you are invaluable, sweet as pie, and, most important, adored by my daughter!

I would like to thank my family, most especially my brother, Michael, who lent his support, his ear, and his love, and who patiently went over every chapter with me line by line, hour after hour, until I felt good enough about it to move on. Putty, you are the wind beneath my wings. I couldn't have written this book without you! And thank you to my sister-in-law, Racquel, not only for putting up with losing Michael for days on end, but for turning into a very good friend.

Lastly, Jon: Thank you for reading every chapter, adding laugh-out-loud jokes, helping immensely with our shorty, never losing your patience with me, and, most important, being so damn good-looking. I won the husband lottery.

CONTENTS

Introduction: Prepartum Obsession   xiii

Love at First Sight   1

Lactose Intolerance   8

The Magic Number(s)   17

Your Baby Doctor   21

Stroller Wars   31

Cheer Up, You Just Had a Baby   41

Cry Baby   52

You'll Never Sleep in This Town
Again   58

The Feeding Frenzy   69

Baby on Bored   78

May I Introduce You to . . . Your
Babysitter   84

Nanny Nurturing 89

Advice: The Good, the Bad, and
the Ugly 95

Developmental Breakdown 102

Your Postbaby Social Life 109

Park Politics 118

Married Mommy, Single Friends 127

Good-bye, Hot Wifey; Hello,
Mommy 136

Taking Off the Baby Weight 146

Mommy and Me, Me, Me 152

Out and About with Your Baby 159

Planes, Trains, and Automobiles 165

Little Brainiacs 172

Women Who Love Their Babies
Too Much 180

Birthday Parties and Other Events
I Don't Want to Be Invited To   186

Name Calling   193

Much Ado About Doo   199

Ain't Misbehaving   204

X-treme Parenting   210

Prepartum Obsession

A few years ago my life changed. My gynecologist told me and my soon-to-be husband that she'd be surprised if I could get pregnant at my late age of . . . midthirties, and with my medical history of pesky fibroid procedures. If I wanted to have a baby, I'd need to get crackin'. She didn't use those words exactly, because she's kind of classy, but I got the message.

And it gave me pause.

It wasn't that I didn't want to reproduce. Of course I did . . . eventually. But this proclamation definitely added some immediacy to the mix.

But the gauntlet had been thrown down, and apparently my husband-to-be and I were up for the challenge, because within a year I was married, a home owner, and pregnant.

With child. Bun in the oven. Bursting with life.

You get the picture.

At first I was thrilled—I'd defied the odds. I was going to be a mother. A mom. Someone's mommy! But as reality set in, questions and doubts started creeping in as well: Would I be a good mom? Am I prepared? Do I have to kiss my old life good-bye? Will I ever want to have sex with my husband again? Will he ever want to have sex with *me* again?

I feared the phenomenon when a perfectly sane woman who swigs Jack Daniel's, never goes to sleep before eight a.m., and has had at least one STD gives birth and suddenly becomes a completely different person. This new "Mommy" personality subscribes to three dozen parenting magazines, thinks a wild night is tossing back two O'Doul's, and never hits the hay after eight p.m.

By the sheer act of having a baby, would I become part of the same cult: joyfully taking classes to learn how to make my own all-organic baby food, wearing turtlenecks in the summer, turning my backyard into a swing set amusement park, and listening exclusively to Top 40?

Would I change into someone I didn't recognize? I might start thinking sex was not something a mommy does, or from now on take only "family vacations" where I'd happily trade in Coronas on a warm beach for LEGOLAND and a local petting zoo.

The thing was, though, regardless of how much I might change, I knew I wanted to be the best mother I could be. I had a chance to make a few wrongs from my childhood right, and to pass a few rights from my childhood on to my own baby. I didn't take this opportunity lightly. But this parenting thing was not my world. I'd never so much as browsed through BabyGap. Plus, my life didn't seem quite set up for a baby. I did have a car with a backseat, but I had very little trunk space. God, I didn't even own a DustBuster.

And since I didn't know many other mothers whom I could use as resources, I started looking into books about pregnancy, caring for newborns, and parenting. There were so many—and they were so varied. Under the avalanche of information, I started worrying more rather than less.

Was there really one right answer? Every book seemed to think so. Did I need to adopt a parenting style? Cloth or disposable diapers? How much should I hold my baby to make sure she felt secure and loved? Was it imperative that I breast-feed until my kid could say "Mom, please put those bad boys away"? Did I need to put my baby on a schedule in order to keep my life the same at all costs—or never go anywhere without my baby and put all her needs way before my own? Should I forgo crib bumpers as if they were the devil incarnate? Could I *ever* use a blanket?

The so-called experts had answers to these questions and many more—so many answers that I found myself completely overwhelmed. Could I decide anything for myself without screwing my child up in some way? In my nervous pregnant state a much needed cocktail was off-limits, but I definitely wanted to lie down for the rest of my pregnancy.

Well, take a deep breath. Now that I have a child (a beautiful, healthy baby girl born November 12, 2004—seven pounds, two ounces, for those who are into that kind of thing) and have spent a considerable amount of time with her, I'm not joining the masses offering you advice. But through my successes, obsessions, and embarrassing confessions I'm prepared to help you sift through the information, and I will attempt to be a voice of reason.

I understand this is a big deal. Whether you got pregnant by "accident" or spent your life savings on fertility treatments, it doesn't change the reality that a baby is a huge responsibility. You've just made the biggest commitment of your life. Having a baby makes buying a house look like a shopping spree at the 99-Cents Only Store. I should know, I've done all three. Your life is about to change drastically. You have invited over a little houseguest, and this little houseguest is never going home—he or she *is* home. Not to mention that this houseguest prefers to wake up at six a.m., no matter how late you kept him or her up the night before.

But take it from my personal experience. If you spend too much time pondering the parenting advice; fretting over every decision; letting other people tell you how to be, feel, and think as a mother, you will have no time to enjoy the very person you're doing all of this for—no, not your mother, your BABY! And your baby is really cute. Go have a look. Visit their little overdecorated room and wake their little butt up. I'm kidding, don't wake your baby up; simply look at him or her through your two-hundred-dollar video monitor. Isn't your baby perfect?

If you could stop worrying about what your baby's eating—or what it's not eating, why you haven't bought him or her a new educational toy in the last five minutes, and whether or not your stroller is hip enough to bring to the parenting competition—you might actually realize that having a baby is pretty darn cool. You'll take in how much you've come to love this creature. This little person who calls you Mommy (or will soon), this brand-new person who needs you like no one has ever needed you before, who brings meaning to your life that you never imagined possible.

Every time you look at your baby's little face, you will see a golden opportunity for videotaping. You will make countless movies that no one would pay admission to see, except you and possibly your very immediate family. So yes, your life will be permanently altered. There really isn't any avoiding it.

My vocabulary is chock-full of baby talk, and I go to more embarrassing lengths than Carrot Top to make my baby laugh. Every decision is now based on what is best for her, and worst of all, my TiVo is filled up with *Dora the Explorer*.

I've been through it and come out the other side. Let me be your guide. Because, yes, I am a changed person.

I care about things like ingredients in cleaning supplies and the dangers of Styrofoam. I know the safety ratings of every brand of car seat, and I spend an inordinate amount of time in sweatpants. But don't write me off yet; I still like to raise hell—just not after eleven p.m.

Love at First Sight

Do you believe in love at first sight? I didn't even fall in love with my husband right off the bat, and believe me, he would be very popular in prison. Yet on our first date I thought he was a little too skinny, WASPy, and young. And now six years later we have a house, a child, and absolutely no closet space, and I love him more than I could have imagined. I think this is the more normal experience. But somehow the media, well-meaning people, and every Sandra Bullock movie ever made have drilled into our heads that this mythical ideal of instant love is better. And this is no truer than when it comes to mother-baby love.

When you're pregnant, people constantly assure you that you will feel this incredible, overwhelming love for your baby, like nothing you've ever known before (clearly most of them have never done ecstasy), the very second your sweet little bundle is placed into your waiting arms. They say that whether you are scared and ill prepared or excited and impatient to be a parent, you will experience this deep unfathomably profound bond right away. Let me take a moment to let you in on a little secret: bullshit. It may happen for a few women, and if it does, fantastic. But it is not a sure thing—far from it. Please don't freak out if your heart doesn't instantly dissolve into love jelly. There's nothing wrong with you. What seems less natural to me is the notion of falling in love with this strange creature so fast.

First off, when that little bun is presented to you fresh out of your oven, you don't even know each other. This is your very first meeting, and it's fraught with incredibly high expectations. That's a lot of pressure. It's like a blind date with a Match.com guy: Up until this point you've only had a rough idea of his height and weight, and a very fuzzy picture to work from. Plus, let's face it, you aren't exactly at your best. You've been in labor, and you are probably under the influence of more drugs than Robert Downey Jr.—which could account for the women who do feel that instant attachment: They're high.

Yes, there are women who report feeling madly in love with their babies the second they lay eyes on them. These women are either very lucky or lying or needy, and I don't trust them. They're the same women who keep a minute-by-minute pregnancy scrapbook, bank cord blood, and name their babies after celebrities. Or maybe they are otherwise normal, but are awash with hormones and narcotics. In any case I have a sneaking suspicion a lot of them will go on to be homeschoolers. But, that said, good for them. I hope their babies don't develop colic. And I mean that sincerely.

The majority of women I've talked to have said that the bonding thing takes time. You have to get to know each other. Go slowly. It certainly doesn't help that before introductions have even been officially made, your baby is already sucking on your breast. Yes, not two minutes into your relationship the little guy's trying to get to second base! Babies are very forward with their needs. Actually, it's kind of refreshing when you think about it. No games.

If you don't fall instantly, madly in love with your baby, don't worry about it. In fact, it might actually be healthier. That way when you do start to feel so strongly attached that your heart might burst, you know it's the real deal.

Personally, I was fully expecting to take one look at my baby and feel the kind of blinding maternal love that you see only in Lifetime movies starring Meredith Baxter. I attribute this either to watching too much cable television or to a study I read on BabyCenter.com that said when you give birth, a chemical, called oxytocin, pumps through your body. (This chemical is not to be confused with OxyContin—but take a moment to think about how great that would be.) This hormone is supposedly so strong it would bring out the mothering instinct in Martha Stewart.

The study goes on to say that as you care for your baby, your body also produces a compound called dopamine. This is a chemical that triggers the reward center of your brain, as heroin or cocaine does. When this chemical is released, it causes you to become "addicted" to your baby. So apparently women who have eight or nine babies are merely chasing the dragon. Ladies, I have a bad feeling there's nothing quite like the initial high. According to the very same study, though, this hormone can be severely dampened by anxiety, fear, postpartum depression, and the thought of your once snug vagina turning into a three-car garage. I guess this bonding thing isn't guaranteed.

When my daughter was handed to me after my C-section, I mostly remember feeling completely over-whelmed. There was relief to have her out of me, fear of actually being this little creature's mother, anxiety of everything that lay ahead, and, oh yeah, I couldn't feel my fucking legs. So, I did cry. Luckily for me I think those tears easily passed for tears of joy.

But this was definitely not love at first sight. I liked my baby right away. I thought she was cute and all, that little nose, oooh and those tiny little hands. But she didn't look even remotely familiar. I needed to get to know her better. Yes, I understood that something momentous had transpired, but I also was in shock and scared about how much my life was about to change.

I couldn't tell you the exact moment I fell hard for my daughter. She simply grew on me every day, and by six months I was definitely her bitch. Some might actually consider me an early bird. I've heard stories from good moms, who, after a few bottles of wine (or as I call it, "therapy"), told me they didn't feel completely bonded until their baby was walking and talking. A couple of these moms admitted that they felt secretly guilty about not intensely bonding right off the bat, because they thought somehow their baby would be able to sense their subtle lack of enthusiasm. Please. As long as you are taking great care of your baby and all of their inestimable needs, they are going to feel loved. Trust me, babies have no idea that while you are sweetly singing them to sleep, you are dying to check your e-mail. No, they're as oblivious as that guy who liked you way too much in high school. Any response on your part will seem hugely encouraging.

Meanwhile, as you're dealing with your little baby day in and day out, ever so slowly the anxiety will wear off. Before you know it, you will start to really enjoy your baby. You'll learn what makes her laugh (fart jokes) and what makes her cry (everything). You will find you have things in common, like your nose and your love of dangly earrings, and you have things that set you apart, like your baby's deeply held esteem for

Raffi. Within days or perhaps months you will find yourself having pangs of love for your child, pangs that make your heart feel like it's in a vise. Yes, at some point you will feel swept up in love. It does happen to every mom, but for some it may take a little longer. Hey, I didn't love *Seinfeld* the first season, and now I TiVo the reruns.

Even if you don't have that instant, all encompassing, magical feeling, it doesn't mean that you don't love your baby. Give yourself a break. But, again, you must trust me on this. Before you know it, you will not even want to imagine what your life was like before this tiny person entered it. Even the toughest cynic will become one of those boring people who say that the best day of their life was the day their baby was born. Or else they'll claim that the best day was when they heard A Flock of Seagulls was mulling over a comeback tour, but the baby day was definitely way up there!

Some Conditions That Can Affect Bonding

Baby's health

Mother's health

Your OB's breath

Uncertainty of father's identity

Postpartum blues

Difficult labor

Missing your prom

Difficult delivery

Colic

Premature baby

Whether or not the baby was planned

Lack of good sitcoms on NBC's fall lineup

Lactose Intolerance

Hi, I'm Stefanie and I'm a bottle-feeder.

If I hear "breast is better" one more time, I swear I'm going to strangle myself with a forty-five-dollar nursing bra. When it comes to your decision on whether or not to breast-feed your baby, way too many people have a strong opinion about what goes on behind your blouse. Some women have even taken to the streets, calling themselves "lactivists," to get every woman on the breast-feeding train and to fight for the rights of breast-feeding women. This can be very irritating, to say the least. Whether you breast-feed or not, you need to be prepared to encounter the Tit Terrorists.

And just know that you will be under surveillance before you've even given birth.

I had no idea when I got knocked up that anyone and everyone would feel the need to weigh in on the tit topic, even in inappropriate places. I've never been one for making a new best friend in the ladies' room, so I was a bit put off when a woman I'd not so much as passed toilet paper to under the stall noticed my obviously pregnant belly and asked me point-blank whether I planned to breast-feed. Not knowing at the time that this was a political hot button, I figured she was simply making unwanted conversation. I innocently answered, "I don't know."

She pounced. "You don't *know*? What do you mean *you don't know*? You absolutely *have* to breast-feed. It's the best thing for your child! If you don't do it, you are robbing your precious baby of the most natural thing in the world." It's like, why bother asking—as if there is an option? You're instantly branded as friend or foe.

She continued lecturing me that not breast-feeding compromises your baby's immune system, causes frequent ear infections, practically ensures obesity, and so on . . . and on and on. Finally I had to interrupt. "Hang on. I didn't mean I don't know if I'm going to breast-feed. I meant, I don't know if I'm keeping the baby." As you probably guessed, that's quite the conversation stopper.

If you want to breast-feed, I think that's heroic. There are, obviously, plenty of great reasons to do it. Word in the ladies' room is that it's the healthiest thing for your baby. A big reason in my book was the healthy part, and that it seemed to be more convenient and a lot less expensive than bottle-feeding. Hell, if I'd known I was going to be a breast-feeding failure, I would've registered for a few tons of Enfamil at my baby shower. So I say give the breast-feeding a try. I want you to succeed. Really.

I also want you to know before going into it what the Breast Brigade probably failed to mention. And that is this: For some women—*most* women—it hurts. Not a little bit: It hurts like a rhesus monkey biting your nipples, only with more screeching—and not coming from the baby. Personally I'm not what you'd call a bondage "enthusiast." I mean, sure I enjoy the occasional nipple clamp, but I'm not a paying member of any bondage club. But if you are going to breast-feed, take a lesson from these experienced folk: You and your baby should work out a "safe" word to deal with this kind of self-imposed pain.

I wanted to breast-feed. But as with everything else, I'd eschewed taking any of the offered breast-feeding classes while I was still pregnant. How hard could it be, right? Wasn't it supposed to be the most natural thing in the world? I tried it in the hospital as soon as I was in my own room, and then every couple of hours afterward, but my baby didn't seem to be taking to it at all. I was getting more and more frustrated, so the nurses sent in the big guns: lactation specialists. Having had that C-section the day before, I wasn't really in the mood for more pain or visitors, but I tried to be open to both. A warning—most lactation consultants have all the charm of a paper cut.

The first woman they sent in had the nonthreatening

name of Cindy and the nonthreatening stature of Webster, but in showing me how to get the "proper latch," she manhandled my breasts until I was in tears. Well, more tears than I'd been in before she came in. Another one showed me the football hold, which required a minimum of twelve pillows and the purchase of a Craftmatic Adjustable Bed. A third woman was named Binky, so I had to disregard what she said, based on her name alone.

Another issue for me was that I was rooming-in at the hospital. This is when the hospital saves money by keeping the baby in the room with the parents the whole time and never in the nursery, where, if you ask me, the baby belongs for at least the first year. To get the baby to stop crying during the night my husband and I desperately made use of all the formula provided to us in the hospital room.

It seems the nurses are on an agenda different from the lactation crew's. For the sake of quiet on the ward the nurses push formula on stricken new parents without mentioning that once a newborn gets a tug of the sweet corporate-brewed formula, most won't want it any other way. Sort of like a Grey Goose rep outside an AA meeting. We also made use of the emergency call button on a number of occasions, and it turns out that "emergency" to maternity ward nurses really means "Maybe I'll pop on by after I finish my sandwich. Or . . . maybe I won't." But that's another topic.

Three days later and armed with too much information, I was sent home before my milk had officially come in. Unfortunately, when I got home, I realized that my baby had the dreaded "nipple confusion." Nipple confusion is when your baby gets a bottle and realizes, "Hey, this is so much easier than trying to suck milk out of a breast that the next time a breast so much as brushes past me, I will scream and scream until either I get a part in Wes Craven's next movie or someone gives me a bottle." It's extremely painful to see your baby refuse your breast, and the only way to combat it seems to be to feed your baby with a dropper until he or she will take the breast again. Taking this approach will leave your baby full and satisfied in slightly under twenty-one hours.

I hired a postpartum doula for my first two weeks home from the hospital. (A doula is a woman hired for an ungodly sum of money to help out during the birth and/or after.) I recommend doing this especially if the new grandparents plan to make themselves scarce until the baby's fortieth birthday. My doula's name was Ofelia, and calling her a breast-feeding fanatic would truly be an understatement. She had raised three boys, all of whom she had breast-fed until they went off to college. And then I'm sure she kept pumping for a while, to be on the safe side. She fully intended to keep me breast-feeding, or to kill all of us trying.

I know that I was hormonal—that was part of it—but

I spent the precious first few days home from the hospital with my brand-new baby crying and crying in frustration and pain. Trying to help me, Ofelia called a previous client who she swore had had a tough time with breast-feeding as well, and put me on the phone with her for moral support. You know when you're talking to a friend on the phone, and they suddenly put their cousin on and say, "Here, talk to Ramona for a minute. She had crabs twice as bad as yours," and you're both dealing with weird silence, but trying to force a little lame small talk? That was me, only shirtless and sobbing on my end. I'm sure this woman was as uncomfortable as I was. She mumbled something supportive, like "Keep doing it or else you are a terrible mom and your baby will wither away."

I *did* keep trying—until my Vicodin ran out. Then all hell broke loose. I cannot believe a loving God intended for us to breast-feed our babies sober. I started to lie to my doula when she came over. I'd say, "Oh, hey, Ofelia! What a coincidence, I just wrapped up a big breast-feeding session! I probably won't need to do it again for a couple of days." Then I'd try once while she was still there, and then wait impatiently for her to leave so I could give my baby a bottle. Not a good use of twenty-four dollars an hour.

My lame attempt at breast-feeding went on for four weeks.

During this crisis I went to see my pediatrician, who asked me how the feeding was going. I burst into tears and told him I was going the breast-feeding route, but having a little bit of trouble.

If you truly want to continue to breast-feed, but are having problems, there is no shortage of help out there for you. Nursing an infant is so complicated that even the most dedicated breast-feeder will probably run into some snafu, like, oh, bloody nipples, which will make them question their sanity. So for the diehards who power on in the face of almost insurmountable pain, I commend you. You don't need this chapter for help, because I'm sure you've been inundated with pro-breast-feeding info since you announced your pregnancy. You can keep reading and laugh at the breast-feeding impaired.

But if you are having trouble breast-feeding and think you may want to stop, you must never call the La Leche League. On their Web site the La Leche League claims that breast-feeding, at its *worst*, can be mildly uncomfortable. Okay, sure, if you consider Nipples Tartare mildly uncomfortable. Know this: The volunteers at this organization have only one purpose and that is to keep women breast-feeding at all costs. They will try to keep you on the phone even when you're done talking to them, until you get the creepy, tingly feeling that they're purposely attempting to keep you on the line, so they can trace the call and dispatch a volunteer to race over and force you to keep trying against your will. Many of these "volunteers" would have you think that not breast-feeding your baby is on par with pulling the plug on Terri Schiavo. If these people could breast-feed other people's babies, believe me, they would.

If you want to stop, it seems no one will step up and tell you that you are not alone. In fact, few people will talk about it at all. Stopping breast-feeding is like getting out of your Columbia Record and Tape Club membership; there are sinister forces at work that don't want to let this happen.

All I can say is, when I sobbed to my pediatrician for the fourth time that I couldn't stop breast-feeding, because I didn't want to be a bad mom and let down my husband, my baby, and my country, and I didn't think I could live with the guilt, he told me to *stop*. And then he assured me that 50 percent of the babies he sees are strictly on formula. Yes, he actually checked his records for me, because I was nearing a nervous breakdown, he's a kind man, and my insurance pays in full. Fifty percent! Yeah, I can do the math! That's half! He then went on to assure me that he hadn't seen any difference in the occurrence of ear infections and obesity, the level of intelligence, and so on, in any of his babies. Yes, I repeat, he said he saw *no* difference. I made him pinky-swear. He reminded me that the most important thing is how the feeding affects your relationship with the baby. Well, let's just say that my baby and I were on the verge of needing counseling.

So, my child has been (Oh-my-god, how could she?) formula fed since she was four weeks old, and she's perfect. Okay, she's not the sharpest tool in the shed, but I blame her father for that, not the lack of breast milk. I hope I don't have to write that I'm KIDDING.

As soon as I stopped breast-feeding, I started enjoying my baby and no longer played possum at feeding time.

I know that most women want to do what's best for their babies. If they don't want to, well, that's a whole different book. But there are a lot of women who can't breast-feed for one reason or another. Some can't for medical reasons, especially breast reduction or breast augmentation. Yup, savor the irony: Pam Anderson's boys probably couldn't feed off those hooters. Some can't tolerate the pain. Others are stressed out, because they're worried they're not making enough milk. Whatever the reason, if you want to continue, then we all support you. But if you want to stop, that's okay too. You shouldn't have to feel like a pariah. No need to wear a big scarlet *F*. There are too many closeted formula feeders. I say we need to be out and proud. We're all doing the best we can. Maybe, someday, we can even have our own parade. Dare to dream.

The Magic Number(s)

When my adorable little sack of suds was only a couple of weeks old, every waking moment (by that I mean every moment, because there was no sleeping going on) felt like I was swimming through cement. The overwhelming majority of advice-givers kept saying, "Wait until your baby is three months old—everything gets a lot easier. She will be a totally different baby." Three months, they chanted, three months. Yup, the second the clock struck three months, I would be witnessing a miraculous turnaround. Everyone said it. Books said it, the dreaded Internet said it, the *Happiest Baby on the Block* guy said it, my hair colorist said it—and that is *so* gospel. Even my own mother was adamant that at three months everything would be better.

Three months seemed to be the magic number. So I waited. I hung on. These people had me thinking my daughter would be gassing up my car and driving my ass to work the second she reached this coveted milestone; that I would be shouting after her, "Wait up for me, silly.

Mommy can't blade THAT fast!" Guess what? They were right. She was a completely different baby.

I'm messing with you. Nothing changed.

I don't know what this whole mystical three-month thing is all about. Perhaps people say it to dangle a carrot in front of you, because they're scared you're so dangerously close to the edge that you're liable to make a break for it, relocate to a nice little ski villa, change your name to Brigitta, and pretend to be single and child-free, leaving those liars to raise your child.

But listen to me. It is NO DIFFERENT AT THREE MONTHS. At three months your baby is still luggage. They're not sitting up, they're not talking or walking or doing any of the chores you've assigned them—no matter how many times you remind them.

But once you pass three months and find out motherhood is not yet a breeze, these same people will promise you a new mystical milestone with such force that you'll fear you will be unprepared. That's right, break out the DV Cam because heeeere comes six months!

Yup, you guessed it, nothing changes drastically at six months either. But the parenting guides try to get you all excited about this age. They say the six-month mark is when you should begin reading books to your baby every day.

I'd been reading books to my baby since before she was born, so this was definitely good news to me. Finally I'd be getting through to her! I pictured myself snuggling with my little sweet pea every night—if you consider five thirty p.m. night, which, as an adult, I certainly didn't use to. As part of our bedtime routine we'd curl up together and pour through the classics. Oh, there would be photo ops galore!

Well, sure enough, my baby seemed to cherish this tradition, not because she liked being read to, but because apparently books are tastier than a frozen Snickers bar. My baby couldn't eat enough books. She ate through Dr. Seuss, *The Red Balloon, The Giving Tree*, and many other pricey hardbacks that had the audacity to be made out of flimsy paper. So to solve this I started giving her a toy to play with while I read the books . . . basically to myself. Good times. Yes, six months is a lot like three months, only with a lot more drool.

One reason that people might tell you it gets easier is that they assume you will begin getting more rest, because your baby will start sleeping through the night. And sure, when your baby does start to sleep through the night, a lot of things will *seem* more manageable simply because you're more rested. But the real reason it gets easier as you go along is *not* because the baby gets easier, it's because you become more accustomed to how insanely difficult the next decade and a half of your life is gonna be. That's 180 months in baby time.

Don't lose hope, though. Babies do eventually get easier, slowly . . . *very* slowly. First they start to smile at you, and that does help. Then they start laughing, and that sound is almost as addictive as online poker. Almost. And then one day before you know it, your baby will be seven years old and going off to overnight camp for the very first time, and you will think, "Wow, it may have just gotten a little easier." And then the camp director will call you at work and say, "Come get your kid because he shot the archery instructor with an arrow" (when the fact is he *grazed* the instructor . . . twice), and you will have to realize it never really gets easy. Only *easier*.

So forget three months, six months, twelve months, or twenty years. Raising your baby is like having your bathroom remodeled. It's a process. For a long while there will be utter chaos, destruction, noise, and bad smells. Every day you will wonder what you were smoking that made you think it was a good idea to redo what had once been a perfectly livable bathroom. For months on end you won't be able to so much as pee without openly weeping. But right when you think you can't live this way another minute, you will suddenly find you have a gorgeous new bathroom, complete with Kohler fixtures exactly as you always dreamed, and you will realize it was all worth it. Even if the final expense ended up being *nine times* the original quote.

Your Baby Doctor

Choosing your pediatrician is an important decision that you will need to make in the months before you pop out your baby. Or so you will be told over and over. I'm certainly not disputing that you should have a pediatrician whom you like and trust. But I do want to say that it shouldn't take a huge chunk of your pregnancy to pick one.

Contrary to what all the books say and what you read on the Web, choosing a pediatrician does not need to be a full-time job. I've heard and read the same advice ad nauseam: Before choosing a doctor for your unborn child, gather a bunch of names, narrow the number of names down to a few dozen, and then interview all of those pediatricians, so you can find one that meets a long list of criteria.

Who has this kind of time on their hands? If you do, then by all means I absolutely recommend that you do this. Make a month of it. Treat it like a trip to Europe; do ten pediatricians in ten days. Have fourteen pages of questions and try to spend an entire day with each doctor. Doctors will love that because they have all kinds of downtime. And when your friends invite you to do something you don't want to do, you have a built-in excuse. "Gee, I'd love to, but I'm doctor hunting. Maybe next year."

Here's the thing: You're not selecting a roommate. Even in bad circumstances you won't be seeing this person every day. They won't be camped out on your couch eating your leftover Thai food and watching *Oprah*. You're going to be seeing them for twenty minutes three times a year, so it's not important that you match every answer on a *Cosmo* magazine compatibility test.

But not only are we supposed to interview a hundred doctors, it seems from the common advice that we're supposed to get right in there and hit them with the tough questions as well. A few recommended questions to ask are:

1. "What do you do to stay current with the latest trends in disease prevention, treatment, nutrition, behavioral problems, and child development concepts, and what type of continuing education do you use?"

This seems like good advice, but *regular people* are supposed to be asking these questions? Most people have trouble asking for a clean fork in a restaurant. I don't think they are going to be up for interrogating their potential pediatrician. Just use your best judgment. If you spot a jar of leeches on the counter or the doctor's big on leprosy vaccines, he's not current.

2. "What philosophy do you follow?"
Listen, Dharma, you're looking for a pediatrician, not a yogi. The philosophy they all follow is "Let's try to keep your baby happy and healthy."

3. "Are you board certified, and do you have a criminal record or a history of malpractice lawsuits, etc.?"
Come on, I know less about my husband.

And then there are a bunch of Nancy Drew detective questions to ask *yourself*:

1. Is the staff at the office friendly and accommodating?
Okay, let's calm down. They're not going to be helping you change a flat tire, they're going to be jotting down a future appointment in their book.

2. If it's a group practice, do you know and like the other doctors?

You have a rich fantasy life if you think you'll be able to interview all the other doctors. You will be lucky if there's enough time to get to yours.

3. Do you have to wait a long time for your appointment?

Now you're delusional. You will never find a doctor's office where the second they see you, they say, "Hey, you! Get in here, silly!" I'd like the whole world to be made of Rocky Road ice cream and Gobstoppers, but that's never going to happen either. Lower your expectations.

4. Is parking plentiful and close by?

Just pick a doctor and stop wasting my fucking time already.

One Web page states that you should get a referral from your OB. I'm gonna have to disagree on this one. Doctors are notorious for recommending other doctors who recommend *them*. Even the best doctors often give mediocre recommendations. If you are going to go this route, make sure that the pediatrician is not just your OB's golf partner, but is someone your doctor has taken his or her own kids to.

I say get a recommendation from someone who lives

near you and has a baby—preferably from a woman who is incredibly high maintenance. This way, you know if the doctor and office can tolerate her insane expectations and hundreds of phone calls after hours, then they will be ecstatic to have you and your baby as patients. At the very least, if your friend is high maintenance, then you know she probably went the "interviewed the hell out of the doctor" route as opposed to the "throw a dart at the pediatrician page of the phone book" route, which would probably have been my fallback. Most people who aren't me have a modicum of sense about them.

Ask your friends how they felt about their pediatricians. They won't hold back the details. Is the doctor compassionate? No matter how many millions of times the doctor has heard the same question before, does he or she act fascinated? Does the doctor give out lollipops after a shot? To the moms?

You'll find a match. When I asked a friendly neighbor of mine what he thought of his child's pediatrician, he said, "We really like him! But you should know: He's really laid back. He never gets fired up over any of the things that we panic about."

Seeing as I'm the sort of person who freaks out a lot over a little, I knew a laid-back pediatrician would be perfect for me. So as soon as my busy schedule of lying around eating pudding opened up a little, my husband and I set up an appointment to "interview" our possible new doctor. We'd put together a lame list of questions that we'd cribbed from the Internet, and we rehearsed them in the car. Plus, we had one other doctor's name on the back burner. But as soon as we met doctor number one, we realized how ludicrous it was to ask all of those canned questions. We liked him instantly and signed up! It was that easy. Done. And we still had time to go home and have sex! Unfortunately, we lacked the motivation.

Our pediatrician, who I won't mention by name because then everyone will want to take their kid to him (check the acknowledgments), was at the hospital every day to see our baby. He did everything short of breast-feeding her.

Yes, the pediatrician was nothing but great. It was my husband and I who ended up being a problem. We needed to learn our office-visit etiquette. And you probably will too.

Seeing as how our first few postbirth office visits were a little unnerving, I bring you this bit of advice on pediatrician protocol. For your doctor's visits you will need to bring a steamer trunk full of baby supplies. I figured since our doctor's office was only blocks away that I wouldn't need to bring anything. Naturally, the second the baby was undressed, she pooped all over the examination table. Hey, cut me some slack, I'd never owned and operated a new baby before. Surprisingly, the nurse seemed underwhelmed when I didn't have a diaper in my pocket, or a wipe or a change of clothes, for that matter. I tried the old "I'm a Christian Scientist and my God doesn't allow me to carry extra diapers," but I guess she'd heard that one a few too many times before. She reluctantly provided us with a newborn diaper, but we had to tote our baby home topless. We'd hoped to avoid *that* scene until at least her first spring break.

Myth: There Are No Stupid Questions

People chant this moronic bromide like a mantra, and nearly always remind you of it when it comes to the pediatrician. No stupid questions? Sure there are! Aren't there stupid questions at your job? Well, then you can reasonably assume there are plenty of questions that work your pediatrician's nerves. That means that you should do your best to avoid asking those questions. That is, if you want to stay on your doctor's "priority appointment list."

You can work on this, but in the beginning put your pediatrician on speed-dial, because you will have a constant barrage of questions and concerns. And some of them are bound to be stupid. A high percentage of those calls will be after hours, because that's the time when you and your baby both get agitated and inconsolable. As far as I know, all doctor's offices take calls after hours. But usually you will have to decide whether your call is an emergency and your doctor ought to be paged right away. This is like asking an alcoholic if they really "need" a drink.

Realizing that you will be interrupting your pediatrician or the on-call partner in the middle of a perfectly good evening at home or, worse, rousing them from a sound sleep, you should try to weed out as many of the stupid questions ahead of time as you can. Of course, a few will slip through.

There was one call to our doctor's office at ten p.m. because our eleven-day-old baby seemed "sleepy." "She's been sleeping a lot," I sobbed to the on-call doctor who'd returned my page before I really hit rock bottom.

"Does she have any other symptoms—fever, diarrhea?" he asked in a not nearly freaked out enough tone for my taste.

"No. But she's really sleeping a lot!"

"Maybe she's tired."

"But it seems like something's wrong."

"Is she having pee diapers?" He definitely wasn't grasping the gravity of the situation.

"Um, yes."

"Then she's probably fine."

"PROBABLY?"

"She's fine. If she stops having pee diapers, then bring her in, but otherwise she's fine."

Obviously I'd pulled this savvy MD out of happy

hour. But short of taking her to the emergency room, I didn't know what else to do but LET HER SLEEP. Little did I know that most women would give up their right ovary to have a baby sleep *at all*, let alone a lot.

Of course, nothing was wrong with my baby, besides her bad mood from my jostling her awake every ten minutes. So, fine, maybe it was a dumb question.

But in the very beginning you will be nervous and want to pose these dumb questions and many more. Your pediatrician should be accommodating.

Keep in mind that all good relationships are based on trust. As anxious as you may be as a new mom, you need to let your doctor do his or her job. Take it on faith that your doctor didn't just transition in to pediatrics from his hosting job at T.G.I. Friday's. Let him take a stab at diagnosing your baby's runny nose before you go and do eight hours of research on the Web en route to your own diagnosis of infant Ebola.

And know that if you find that your pediatrician isn't taking your real concerns seriously, or you feel uncomfortable in any way, or your doctor suddenly has some mysterious malpractice suit pending, you have my permission to switch doctors. Yes, you can do this. We live in a country where there is no shortage of MDs. You can single-handedly keep Harvard Medical

School in business if you choose to—no explanation needed. But remember the most important question to ask when you're interviewing them is, "Do you take my insurance?"

Stroller Wars

The quest for baby goods blossoms for a lot of women while they're still in early pregnancy. It's as if the fertilized egg is the starter gun for a stampede of consumerism that will last for decades. These days some people fork out a lot of cash on imported German strollers, overpriced outfits from stores with names like Monsieur Cranky Pants, and toys—more cash than Joan Rivers spends on eye lifts.

I ran into one of these ladies at my OB's office. I had been scanning the waiting room, hoping to find someone to talk to who at least had a little bit of personality, so I struck up a conversation with the only woman not knitting. She immediately tried to engage me in a discussion about nursery themes. Up until that moment I honestly hadn't known nurseries had themes. It's a baby's room, not Disneyland. But I guess having a crib and a lamp just isn't enough. Nowadays you have to have an authentic jungle theme or a fairy princess theme, complete with bamboo or castles. There are actually dozens of books devoted entirely to this subject. Go to Amazon.com, type in "baby nursery," and then promptly kill yourself. There's even one called *Nursery Décor*. I'm sorry, but easy on the décor! Babies don't even see in color until they're, like, teenagers or something.

If you want to spend thousands of dollars filling your baby's nursery, that's up to you, I guess, but your baby's not going to appreciate that you bought a crib that matches the dresser and changing table, plus a valance that perfectly coordinates with the sheets. I think what's more important are the things that either save you time or keep you from losing your mind. Retaining your time, your sanity, and a little spending scratch will probably make a more lasting impression on your child than auditioning for the next edition of *Nursery Décor Idol*. So let me steer you toward what you can't do without.

Make Room for Baby

We'll start with the star attraction in any baby's nursery. That's right, monitors. Some people get the video monitors so they can keep an eye on their baby, as though they're working the night shift at 7-Eleven and their baby's a potential shoplifter. This seems like an unhealthy endeavor to me. If you're not careful, monitor abuse can become a full-blown addiction. A quick peek can turn into two hours of continuous screening, and before you know it, you're calling in sick to work, so you can get *one more look*, just one more. Trust me, it's not worth it.

Plus, in the beginning, the times that your baby is sleeping and you're awake are few and far between. Do you really want to waste these rare opportunities *watching* your baby? You two spend enough time together. Now step away from the monitor and go do something productive . . . like watching television.

Actually, I probably shouldn't laugh at other people's monitor obsessions, since I myself bought the one that monitors the baby's breathing. It sounds an alarm if it detects no motion for fifteen seconds. I found it to be a wonderful alternative to tiptoeing into her room and holding a mirror in front of her little nose every ten minutes throughout the night. But I'm a little unbalanced. Moving on.

As for cribs, I don't care what kind you get, but do yourself a favor and get the crib bumpers. I know you may have been notified that you shouldn't have crib bumpers now, it's the latest scare. (Although by the time you read this the latest study may say that crib bumpers are the only thing proven to raise your kid's IQ.) My husband and I, paranoid first-time parents that we were, took a safety course for infants and came away with all sorts of new fears. The biggest one was that our baby would surely suffocate if we put crib bumpers in her crib. The bumper police had us convinced that babies' faces are drawn to bumpers like Tara Reid is to apple martinis. It's absurd.

Take it from me: You need crib bumpers, and not only because they look cute with your choo-choo train crib sheets. You need crib bumpers so your little baby doesn't get his little leg stuck through the bars of the crib, or bump his head against the rails like a mental patient in a *SpongeBob SquarePants*–themed institution. Plus, with no bumpers your crib will look barren. Nothing is sadder than looking through those bare bars, like it's visiting hours at the state prison. Believe me, that will come soon enough.

If you're scared of bumpers, chances are you also think blankets in the crib are the Antichrist. You should know that a lot of people swear by them for their warmth and cuddle factors. If you're really worried, try a crocheted blanket. Even your little genius will never figure out how to suffocate in that.

But I accept that with the level of paranoia these days, some people won't relax unless their baby is completely naked, sleeping on a fully enclosed cement slab with no teddy bear in sight. Good luck with that.

Infan-tainment

There's no excuse for your living room looking like Romper Room . . . at least when company comes by. The rest of the time it will be inevitable. Before I had a baby, like a lot of childless women I would wince when entering the home of a parent. It seemed so babycentric and unfun. (Is "unfun" even a word? I think once you have a baby, you are allowed to use the word "unfun" as often as you want, or at least as frequently as other people use the word to describe you.) But now I wince when people without children drop by unexpectedly.

For the first few years of your baby's life your house will be chock-full of baby crap, and you are going to need every bit of it. Simply surrender to that notion now, if you want to save your last bit of sanity. And know that it's only for the first year or so that your living room will look like this, because when your baby becomes a small child, it will look much, much worse. Even though you can't do without most of this stuff, you might want to have an escape route from it when you have company—maybe a spare bathroom that you can pretend is off-limits. Then throw all the stuff inside when people come over who need a place to actually set a drink down.

Rest assured, even if you naively attempt to streamline the clutter, there are a couple of things you *must* have.

A lot of parents love to swing. I mean, love *the* swing. They swear it's the only thing that helps give them a few extra minutes' sleep in the morning or the ability to unload the dishwasher. From what I hear the majority of babies find the swing more sleep-inducing than Tylenol PM, which can make the swing worth its weight in gold. Turned out my baby was in the minority on this one. But, lucky for me, I bought mine used and passed it on to another hopeful mom.

Now, the Gymini is a horse of a different color—or, more precisely, a great many different colors. This god-send is a brightly colored mat with a felt arch from which you can hang different toys. At first glance a Gymini may not seem like a must-have. But it is, my friend. Seriously, what the heck do you think babies do in the first few months but lie on their backs and stare at shit? This thing is a bargain at about fifty bucks. Pink Floyd's *The Wall* and laser light show not included.

Next you will need to get yourself an ExerSaucer. This is an activity center that your baby hangs out in for longer periods of time than you imagined possible, swiveling around to play with an array of different toys. It may be your most important purchase. I say register for one at your baby shower, because these bad boys are overpriced. Once you see what they're made of, you will be pretty sure you could have built one yourself for about two dollars and change. But since you aren't going to have time to bleach your mustache, let alone build an ExerSaucer from scratch, prepare to shell out the money if no one else springs for it.

And be sure to pick a time to put this thing together when you're not working through any major issues in your life. If it seems like the directions are written in Japanese, it's because they are. So for a slightly easier time, you may want to check out the English directions written handily on the last page. Once you get the thing set up, though, it will be like Christmas morning. Not for the baby, but for you! You will have your hands free for possibly the first time since you had the baby! I think this thing is a must-have, and anyone who tells you it's a luxury item probably considers heart medication a recreational drug.

You'll want to break it out when your baby is about four months old. The box says five months, but you'd have to have the patience of a Saint Bernard to wait that long, and your baby will probably want nothing more to do with it by the time she's about nine months old. So, don't screw around. You have a short but wondrous window of opportunity.

By the way, the ExerSaucer is not meant to be a substitute for paying attention to your baby. But provided you're not leaving your kid in there by themselves while you hightail it to Vegas for a few hands of blackjack, there's no harm in letting them entertain themselves for a while as long as they're happy.

Once your baby gets used to it, it will be like her own home. You can put her in it while you do the dishes, check your e-mail, or even run out to the gym. Hey, calm down, I'm kidding. I'm sure you're not motivated enough to go to the gym.

Road Rage

I don't know what it is about having a baby that makes certain women immediately get on the phone with the good people at Hummer to ask if they're going to be coming out with something a tad larger. I personally don't think you need an SUV the size of Brazil to take your kid to soccer practice. But if you must have one, get one. I don't care anymore. I give up. You win. You rule the road. Only, please spare me the BABY ON BOARD sign. God, I pray you at least have a dog in there to justify this waste of space.

Speaking of moving vehicles, not only are car seats superconvenient, but they are the law in every state. Well-meaning folks who want you to spend a lot of money will tell you to buy only a brand-new one. But if you know for a fact that it's never been in an accident, I don't see any harm in using your sister-in-law's, as long as it hasn't been stored in her basement since parachute pants were cool.

There are different types of car seats. You will probably first buy the infant car seat. This one is good because you can haul it around with you and put it in shopping carts, on bus seats, on top of washing machines, etc. Once your baby is more than about twenty pounds, you will need the convertible. And let me recommend getting it professionally installed, if you don't want to go through a trial separation from your husband for an entire weekend, after fighting about whether he installed it correctly.

Even if you're not into attachment parenting, you will need an infant carrier. The BABYBJÖRN seems to be what most people get; in fact, the term is almost a verb now: to Björn. As in, I'm going to Björn it for my trip to Mommy & Me yoga. The Björn is great until Mama's little fatty gets to be about sixteen pounds, and then, not so much, unless you're into visiting the chiropractor twice a week. Yes, I've read the fine print, and I know they hold up to twenty-five pounds, but I have never witnessed anyone wearing a baby that big. A rule of thumb is: If you can't figure out who should be carrying whom, it's time for a stroller.

The stroller, in fact, will be one of your bigger purchases. If you have $729 to throw around, you could buy yourself a Bugaboo, since the Bugaboo stroller has replaced the Peg Perego as the de rigueur brand for competitive mommies. Or you could donate that money to help a poor family get their oldest child a few extra sessions on dialysis. But that's your call. Madonna owns one, and she has a fake British accent, so I guess that proves they're worth it.

I've seen a lot of strollers in my day, and I haven't seen that big a difference between them. But that's just me. As long as it has wheels and you can still manage to fold it up after a couple of mimosas, you should be fine.

The biggest truth you will learn about baby paraphernalia—regardless of whether you prespend the college education fund—is that you will never have enough. There will always be something new and there will always be something better. And every day you will realize something that would make your life totally workable if only you had it. But the joy is that you will need to come up with reasons to get out of the house, anyway. So now you'll have an excuse. You need more stuff. Always. More. Stuff.

Cheer Up, You Just Had a Baby

A lot has been said and written about postpartum depression. And although researchers believe that depression is one of the most common complications during and after pregnancy, it looks like no one knows exactly what causes it. It seems to stem from a drastic change in hormone levels, but a lot of intangible factors come into play. It's kind of like gingivitis; no one knows exactly what the hell it is, but we know we don't want to get it. Mostly we hear about the extremes of depression—either the whisper of despair known as "baby blues" or the "drown your kids" postpartum psychosis. But let me tell you from personal experience, there's a whole world of in-between, and none of it's pretty.

I, like most women, had heard of baby blues but wasn't terribly worried about it, mainly because it sounds like a cute disorder, one you could hug away in a day or two. Hell, it even has a sweet name that could be a description for an adorable baby outfit or a beautiful eye color. In fact, I'd even secretly looked forward to it. Who couldn't use a day of ice cream and Nora Ephron movies?

Little did I know, the baby blues are not cute—unless you consider it "cute" to alternate for days on end between crying and carbo-loading.

Most women envision their postbirth experience as being the most beautiful time of their lives. I've yet to meet anyone whose *actual* experience lived up to their expectations, and this buildup can lead to a fall.

I imagined that I'd be all glowing and mellow during the weeks after delivering my baby. I thought it was within my grasp, seeing as how incredibly serene I felt through most of my pregnancy. This had to be due to pregnancy hormones. Nine weeks into my pregnancy the morning sickness was gone and I was feeling fine—better than fine. Luckily, the same pregnancy hormones that cause you to feel crappy in the beginning can actually make you feel good once your body adjusts to them. I felt calm. If you didn't know me, you might mistakenly think I was into meditation or something. One friend said, "Wow, you're really doing great, considering that your life is about to change so drastically. I get nervous when I try a new shade of toenail polish."

I smiled smugly. "I guess I'm good with change." I was actually under the hormonal delusion that I had a laid-back personality.

Like many women, I had a lot of great soft-focus

fantasies about how utterly sweet life would be once the baby got here. Self-confidence would be oozing through my pores, and my maternal instinct, along with that hour-and-forty-five-minute infant-care class I took, would help me "just know" how to do everything. I envisioned myself lying in bed, cuddling and nursing my new baby, the poster child for breast-feeding. Naturally, there would be a parade of well-wishers who would stop by and be astounded by how quickly I'd bounced back from giving birth. In fact, we all would look so good that a famous photographer would be dropping in to shoot a photo spread of my newly formed family for *Greatest Parents Ever!* magazine.

Interestingly, not one of my Earth Mother fantasies had me home from the hospital a week after giving birth, more bloated than a professional bowler, with dark circles under my eyes, and sobbing nonstop all day long on the couch. Yet that would be the more accurate picture.

After you give birth, no matter how excited you were and still are, your body goes through changes and your hormone levels drop from the highest they've ever been to completely down off the charts.

Once those hormones took a nosedive, so did my mental health. I've never felt as bad as I did during the days following "the happiest day of my life." After the initial awe of having a child came the overwhelming realization that her life was in my hands. All day long I was petrified that something was wrong with my baby.

I'd stare at her while she slept peacefully, willing her to wake up so I'd know she was okay. Positive that she wasn't breathing properly, I counted her breaths using a stopwatch, and convinced myself that her complexion looked bluish.

While worrying incessantly about the baby, I also knew with certainty that my husband was plotting his escape. I didn't blame him one bit. I wouldn't want to live with me either. I was a complete mess. Besides greeting each new day with constant crying, I was still fifty pounds overweight and I had cellulite *on my arms*, for Christ's sake.

To be fair, I'd been prone to little bouts of relationship paranoia in the past. Like when my husband and I were first dating. After any large or small disagreements I found it comforting to have a nice four-hour marathon talk to really be sure we'd smoothed things over. A lot of men, I realized, only like to have *two-hour* talks—three, tops. And if there's a shark special on The Discovery Channel, they may want to forgo conversation altogether. So, okay, I'd always suspected that I might be a teensy bit emotionally high maintenance, but I chalked it up to being "artistic." And, to my credit, after the first year of dating I chilled out a lot.

Well, here we were almost six years later, and within forty-eight hours I'd slid so far down that I made Anna Nicole look emotionally stable. I figured my husband was about two crying jags away from leaving me to find a new mother for his baby: someone thin, cute, dry-eyed, and maybe, oh, eight years younger than me.

My husband attempted to reassure me, but he didn't know what to do. He tried telling me that what I was feeling was probably caused by hormones and was completely normal. Of course, in my mind this was akin to him saying "Isn't your period about due?" and I didn't respond well. He even offered to take the baby into another room overnight and to be responsible for all the feedings, so that I could get some much-needed sleep. I know, I know, most new mothers would happily give up Splenda for a year in exchange for one decent night of sleep, but I accused my husband of wanting to be away from me.

Finally he begged me to please tell my obstetrician what was going on.

The moment my doctor walked into the examining room at my first postpartum checkup, I started crying. I guess there was no real reason at that point to ask "How are you feeling?" But my outburst didn't even knock the doctor off his script. He nonchalantly said, "Go ahead and get dressed and come into my office."

With pants back on and tears still a-streamin' I explained to him how awful I was feeling. "I can't sleep, I'm crying all day long, and I'm sure my husband has his bags packed. I'm taking care of my baby, and I love her, but I'm feeling completely overwhelmed."

All he said was, "Well, you just had a baby. It's a big responsibility."

"This feels like a little more than that," I said.

"Yes, well, it sounds to me like a touch of the baby blues."

This was "a touch" of the baby blues? It felt more like the display at Costco had just collapsed on my head.

"It's perfectly normal, nothing to worry about," he reassured me. "You'll be fine. If you're not feeling better in a couple of weeks, then let me know and we can write you a prescription for something."

I prayed that "something" would be a morphine drip.

He continued, "If I write you a prescription for something today, by the time it starts working, you'll already be feeling better."

I knew if I tried to argue there'd be more tears, so I opted to take his word for it and went home to white-knuckle it out.

During a subsequent bout of insomnia I did some Internet research and found that baby blues occur in 50 to 80 percent of women within the first few days of giving birth, and may last for a few days or a few weeks. Baby blues are described as weepiness, anxiety, and emotional instability. The feelings should get increasingly less intense, often resolving themselves within a few weeks.

According to my personal research here's what having the baby blues is *not*: It's not feeling a little overemotional; it's not getting misty-eyed at a sappy AT&T commercial; it's not bursting into tears because you spotted a rainbow.

Baby blues are also not "a lot like PMS," as I've seen it described in some books—although I know that some women have murdered their husbands and successfully used the PMS Defense, so maybe I'm underestimating bad PMS.

The baby blues are BLUES. That's the reason the condition is called "baby *blues*" and not "baby *a little over-emotional.*" It's sadness. You're sad. And you think you're not supposed to be sad, because you just had a baby and that's supposed to make you feel happy and complete. So you leap to the conclusion that you must be a bad person.

Women experience postpartum depression in varying degrees. Mine was a pretty rough experience. A percentage of new moms don't get any depression at all. These are the same women who never suffer cramps with their periods, never experience the blinding pain of a migraine, and never had someone break up with them through e-mail. These are the sort of women who enjoyed junior high school. Feel free to resent them; everyone else does.

Some other women had such miserable pregnancies that simply having the baby out of them feels like a European vacation. I cut those women a lot of slack.

But there is another type of woman who insists she had a wonderful pregnancy and doesn't believe in postpartum anxiety. This type of woman refers to her baby's birth as "the blessed event" and throws around the word "amazing" like Jay-Z uses "bitch." If you're suffering from baby blues, this woman will only compound your anxiety by constantly reminding you of how "ecstatic you should be feeling!" and how "mommy time is a gift to be treasured every second of every day!" and how you should be getting up off that couch and shouting from the rooftops, "Thank God Almighty, I'm a mommy at last!"

Just know that this woman is in denial. She is the type of woman whose husband is sleeping with her best friend, but she chalks up all their late nights together as "They must be planning a surprise party for me." Uh-huh. For the past three years? Yeah, that'll be one hell of a surprise!

Two weeks after my initial doctor's appointment I went back for my follow-up. I was still crying more than a drunk sorority chick at a pinning ceremony. I gave him the "no change" update.

He said, "You should be fine in about two weeks."

What? "You said that last time, and two weeks later here I am."

"Oh, okay, well, then let's get you on an antidepressant and see how it goes." He said it like it had just that second occurred to him.

So I was sent home with a prescription for Paxil. I'd already had the prescription filled and I'd popped a pill before even pausing to read the instructions. If I had read the information, I would've seen the small print where it mentioned a .0001 percent chance of mania in new users. Guess who was that one ten thousandth of a percent? Yup, I was flying.

Luckily, I was scheduled to attend a neighborhood cooking club that night (in spite of the fact that I rarely cook and don't intend to start), and let me tell you, these women could use a dose of mania. Even a well-steeped cup of English breakfast tea would help liven up this group. I told tales a mile a minute of my five-week-old daughter, my postpartum depression, my love of ABBA, and my trouble breast-feeding. The mommies stared at me as though I'd suggested we all swap husbands for the night.

I called my mother at midnight (which should've been her first clue something was off) to tell her how fantastic I felt. She told me to stop taking the Paxil immediately. At least I think that's what she said. When I tried calling back a few dozen times for clarification, she'd turned her ringer off, so we'll never know for sure.

Before I had a chance to go back to the doctor to get on the antidepressant option number two, I noticed I was starting to feel better. I had stopped breast-feeding, which evened out my hormones; I started exercising; my husband was taking some middle-of-the-night feedings; and I was talking to other mothers about how I felt. This is key. Pretty soon I was down to merely constant complaining, which actually wasn't too far from my normal state of being. And eventually I was dealing with the adjustment to parenthood rather than the actual depression, which was a hell of a lot better. Plus, I sold the rest of my Paxil to a bipolar friend for a nice profit. So it was a win-win situation.

No matter what, you're going to have feelings flying at you from every direction, and if you're prone to anxiety, I'd bet my baby you'll get some form of postpartum depression. As it turns out, I was one of the lucky ones. Some women who get more serious postpartum depression can get all these symptoms and worse.

One normally sane and loving woman I know called me one day, crying, when her child was six months old and told me that she was having thoughts about hurting her baby. She said, "I'd never in a million years do it, but I'm obsessed with what would happen if I dropped him, and I keep picturing it in my mind." Hello, red flag! Please don't let it get this bad.

Everyone experiences some type of emotional response to the drastic plunge in hormone levels. You've also just had a baby and your life is very suddenly, very drastically, changed forever. That's some heavy shit that can't help but change you in a permanent way. I challenge you to find a new mother, or *any* mother, whose eyes remain dry while watching a newscast involving a baby. It doesn't even have to be a human baby. Chimps, llamas, even hamsters will bring on the tears.

But if your feelings get out of control or if you experience depression for more than a couple of weeks, you probably need help to get over it. Hell, I need help to cope when I have no new messages on my voice mail, so there is nothing wrong with seeking medical attention for depression. However, if you find that you're feeling tired all the time, you're overwhelmed and irritable, and you have virtually no sex drive whatsoever, welcome to motherhood, my friend.

Cry Baby

It's inevitable. Your baby will spend a lot of time crying. Possibly not as much as you will if you're suffering from postpartum depression or if it's only now sinking in that you may never see a nonelastic waistband again, but without fail your kid is destined to log countless hours of tears. And never before has any one sound felt as soul piercing, heartbreaking, earth-shattering, and irritating all at the same time. Your baby's cry is primal.

Women are incredibly sensitive to the sound of their baby's cries, which is exactly how nature intended it. Unless you've popped a prescription horse tranquilizer, your baby's cry will draw you in like a magnet—from an engrossing dream about Orlando Bloom, from the shower, or from twenty thousand leagues under the sea. It's almost impossible for a woman to carry on with a normal activity while her baby's wail floats overhead like the Goodyear blimp, announcing in a blinking bright red message: I need you, MOMMY!

But why does your baby need you at that particular time? That's the sixty-four-thousand-dollar question. According to the paranoia-inducing early-child-development books that we moms seem to pore over obsessively, by the time our babies are a few weeks old, we should be able to read their cues and discern their needs from the sound of their cries. This is a load of crap.

Babies are not like phones. They don't have different ring tones to warn you when it's important (hunger) or tell you when you should let it go to voice mail (bored, tired). Other than a cry of pain, which is hard to miss—like when my baby slams her finger in a drawer, or her delicate ears hear the word "no"—I still can't always tell the difference. And I don't know any other mom who can honestly do it either.

Crying is like a foreign language. And since you don't speak Baby and it's not taught in any accredited universities, it will be faster to wait for them to learn yours. Yes, I know Daryl Hannah learned to speak English in *Splash* from watching TV over a long weekend. But you can't compare yourself to that. She was a mermaid, and mermaids have a real ear for languages. So, until your little one develops some communication skills and can explain what's wrong, you'll have to attempt to figure it out.

At first when your baby cries, nine times out of ten you'll find it's because they're hungry, and even on the one in ten chance that hunger isn't the problem, feeding them certainly can't hurt. Cure all: no. Mood enhancer: absolutely. Besides hungry, your baby could be tired, bored, stressed, teething, too hot, too cold, going through a nasty breakup—the list is endless. This is when you have to follow the clues to find your culprit. Did baby skip a nap? You don't have to be Lieutenant Columbo to realize that Mr. Sandman might've set off your baby's delicate car alarm. Of course, it's not always that simple.

I'll never forget one particular afternoon when my daughter was about eight months old. She cried for at least two hours off and on, for no reason I could suss out. I went through my checklist. She'd already eaten about ninety minutes before, and I'd changed her diaper so many times that day I was developing carpal tunnel syndrome, so that wasn't it. Could her little gums hurt? I gave her Motrin (otherwise known as baby crack) just in case. No help. Was she bored? I played and sang to her, popped in a video, tried hugging it out, and even busted out my best Michael Flatley "Lord of the Dance" imitation, but her bad attitude persisted. After two hours I was ready to auction her on eBay. Luckily, no one met my reserve, or I would have had a bit of explaining to do to my husband.

So while she continued to cry, I pondered the situation over a nice cool glass of Diet Coke. That's when it occurred to me that she might be thirsty, considering that she'd eaten a salty hot dog for lunch. I offered her some juice and she dove on the sippy cup, taking a huge relieved swig as though she were Courtney Love on her first day out of rehab. I guess I should've been pleased, but I completely lost it, the tears started rolling. What was wrong with my parenting skills? How could it have taken me two hours to think of *thirsty*! That's, like, Mothering 101.

Of course, in the big scheme of screwing up, that was amateur stuff. You'll get used to falling short of your mothering ideals time and time again. Give yourself a break. They're babies, they can't talk yet! Despite what the books claim, for a long time, when your kid is teary, it will take trial and error to figure it out. But you'll do it because the motivation will be there driving you. This is exactly why letting-the-baby-cry techniques are too difficult for most moms. The sound is almost physically painful, and you will feel driven to find the reason for it and to help it stop. Imagine if a man with a brand-new Porsche had to listen to his car alarm going off right outside his window and do nothing about it. He'd be in therapy for a year.

So go through that mental Rolodex of possible causes a couple of times, and you should be able to solve most situations. Eventually.

Unless your baby is colicky. Then you're going to be in a pickle.

The clinical definition of colic is: A condition of early infancy marked by chronic irritability and crying—

so much crying that you may be tempted to commit a major felony in order to get some much-needed quiet time in the comfort of a federal penitentiary. *Webster's* may have something different, but they're a little out-dated.

A colicky baby is a force to be reckoned with. Babies with colic can cry for three hours or more a day at least three times a week, seemingly for no reason. It usually appears in babies when they're two to three weeks old, reaches its peak at six weeks, and is done after three or four months—much like most of my relationships in my twenties. Apparently there is nothing you can do to cure it. Isn't that amazing? Scientists have found a way to remove all the fat from potato chips, yet they can't get a colicky baby to stop howling for a half hour. It doesn't seem fair. And every suggestion about how to help them stop crying, short of general anesthesia (for you), seems too soft to yield any lasting results.

I'll list them anyway, just in case. Some remedies include: swaddling, putting her in the baby swing, running the vacuum, going for a car ride, giving her a warm bath, giving her a pacifier, giving her a tummy rub, going for a walk, putting in heavy-duty earplugs. You'll find most of these remedies as effective as trying to soothe a compound fracture with Advil. Yeah, they won't work too well on your run-of-the-mill babies, let alone on Old Yeller.

Remember that no matter what you do or don't do,

in a few months your little one will be fine as wine. And, seeing as how babies have no short-term memory, they'll have no recollection of their weeks and weeks of misery and constant screaming.

Luckily, you'll be able to tell them all about it.

You'll Never Sleep in This Town Again

You want your baby to sleep. I understand that. I want your baby to sleep too. Hell, deep down even your baby wants to sleep. But we all need to back away from the baby and take five deep breaths when it comes to this highly charged subject. Your child's sleep or lack thereof may have nothing to do with what you are or aren't doing. Babies are all individuals, and they have minds and circadian rhythms all their own. If your baby isn't sleeping, the problem may lie more with your reaction than with the baby itself.

Anywhere new mothers are gathered you will hear phrases like "family bed" and "Ferberizing" spoken about in hushed tones. These regimens are often discussed with the electric mix of hope and despair associated with a life-long chubber who first hears about Jenny Craig.

The danger is, the sleep-deprived new mother's desperation for answers can make her vulnerable to the slew of self-appointed "sleep experts" who are hell-bent on advocating what they know to be the *only* answer.

Some people will claim it's all about the bedtime ritual, while others will convince you that if there's no set schedule all day, you're doomed. Most people swear that without *their* method you can forget about you or your child ever having a decent night's sleep. Sorry to be a buzz kill, but nobody except you is an expert on your baby.

Even if your baby is already sleeping through the night, it won't be quick enough for the "sleep experts." I was in line at Costco, picking up another U-Haul full of supplies for my daughter, when a woman with crazy eyes, who looked like she hadn't slept a wink since the early nineties, stepped into line behind us with an infant in a carrier. Following new-mommy protocol, I asked how old her baby was, and she told me two months. Then she asked how old my baby was, and I said four months. We were off to the races. New mom immediately asked, "Is she sleeping through the night?" to which I answered truthfully, "Yes, thank God."

"Reeeeally. How long has she been doing it?"

"Umm . . . she's actually been sleeping through the night fairly consistently since she was about three months old."

She looked at me with a mix of condescension and pity, as though I were a mixed breed puppy in the pound, sooo cute but not quite what she had in mind. "My baby's been sleeping all night since he was nine days old. You should really pick up this fantastic book called something like *My Baby Started Sleeping Through the Night Before Your Baby."*

What part of "OUR BABY IS SLEEPING THROUGH THE NIGHT" did this bizzotch not understand? If her book were going to be useful to me, she'd have to recommend a good one on time travel too.

I gave her my best "good luck with your mental illness" smile and hightailed it out to the parking lot.

Up until that moment I had been feeling great about my baby's sleeping habits. Not only because my baby now seemed to appreciate sleep almost as much as I did, but mostly because my husband and I had suffered so much before she got the hang of it.

Early on my daughter had her days and nights mixed up, as a lot of babies do. But then it got worse instead of better. She slept all day, and by eight o'clock at night she was wide awake, ready to throw down. She grew progressively more alert the later the hour became. The more alert she became, the more horrified and sleep deprived we became. My husband and I blamed ourselves. Could it be in the genes? Before she came along we'd always been big night owls, never having dinner before ten and happily staying up until three a.m. to catch the newest Bo-Flex infomercial. But now we honestly couldn't keep up with her. She had taken on the lifestyle of a New York club kid, clearly having contempt for people who went to bed before dawn. I tried to shift myself to her daytime sleep schedule, but it worked about as well as the afternoon I tried to become a vegetarian.

By the time she was about seven weeks old, we were at the end of our rope. Getting almost no sleep at all for weeks on end, we were starting to turn on each other.

We waited for our next appointment with the pediatrician like we were waiting to receive the Holy Grail. Surely he'd make it better. When the day of our visit came, we presented our baby to him like she was a busted VCR. "Can you fix it, please? We can't seem to set the clock." We explained the situation, and when we got to the part about her not falling asleep until the wee hours of the morning, he looked a bit worried.

"Hmmm. She should really be going to sleep by about nine thirty at her age."

I looked back at our doctor. "Nine thirty, huh? I guess we read the wrong book, 'cause we thought THREE A.M. was a more appropriate time for a baby to go to sleep. Can't you tell by the hollow, soulless looks on our faces what a treat this is for us?" Then I had to stop and get ahold of myself. Whoa, I must have been more sleep deprived than I'd thought—to snap at my doctor like this. My husband's one thing, but I really liked my doctor.

"You know, it's okay to let her cry for a few minutes," our doctor offered, seemingly unfazed by my outburst.

"How long is 'a few minutes'?" I asked. We actually hadn't considered that yet.

"It won't hurt her to cry for ten minutes or so. But

don't let her cry for a long time at her age. She's too young." That wouldn't be a problem, seeing as how I'd rather be forced to look at pictures of Rush Limbaugh naked than leave my two-month-old baby to scream.

He said, "Don't worry. She'll figure it out."

Letting other people figure things out for themselves has never been my strong suit. And now was not an optimum time for self-improvement. I knew it would be a lot faster for me to figure it out myself and then let her know what she was doing wrong.

I found that there are a lot of different methods that people use to get their babies to sleep. Different ones work for different people, and some of them work for no one except the childless sadists who conceived of them.

One of the biggies is Dr. Sears's school of thought, which is in essence that kids sleep better in bed with their parents. Yeah, well, the babies may sleep like . . . babies, but the parents sleep like they're taking the bar exam the next day. We'd already tried this method, without knowing it was a method someone makes money from.

In the first few weeks home our new spawn refused to sleep anywhere but in bed with us. She was having none of the adorable bassinet, decorated in the pink etoile (a word I'd only recently learned the definition of) I'd so carefully chosen. She screamed the second she was placed down onto its plush sixteenth of an inch of plastic padding, like she was being lowered onto hot coals, which inevitably forced us to bring her into bed as a last-ditch option. But, despite Dr. Sears's opinion, having a seven-pound baby in a bed with two adults was far from relaxing; it was like trying to snuggle with a Ming vase. We kept an all-night semiconscious vigil, petrified of falling fully asleep and mistakenly rolling over onto her. After a few nights and zombie days of this we were ready for *any* alternative.

P. T. Barnum said there's a sucker born every minute, and I'd bet most of those are gullible parents trying to get a newborn to sleep. Endless pricey appliances are perched on the shelves of every baby store, simply waiting for sleepy parents to stumble into range. My husband, on a desperate run to Babies "R" Us, took the bait with something cloyingly named the Snuggle Nest. This thing is basically a postal service crate that shamelessly retails for fifty bucks. It fit into the middle of our queen-size bed, leaving each of us a leftover place about the size of a Post-it note to sleep. That item lasted until the opening credits of Conan O'Brien and has been collecting dust under our bed ever since. I seriously think we narrowly escaped at least one of us needing back surgery.

Okay, to be fair, some people who aren't me swear by the family bed. I think that's great if you can and want to sleep that way. But if I may, a word of caution: Once your child gets used to sleeping in your bed with you, they won't want any part of their own room and own crib. So, you need to be committed to doing the family bed at least until your baby's a teenager, or until it destroys your marriage.

On the opposite end of the scale we have the hardcore "sleep trainers." When people think of sleep training, most think of Dr. Ferber's method—also known as "Ferberizing." It's one of the techniques that prescribe letting babies Cry It Out (CIO). Ferber preaches that some babies older than six months need to "tough it out" and learn to self-soothe. He recommends putting them down awake and allowing them to cry for longer and longer periods of time each night before you briefly go check on them.

Personally I have nothing against Dr. Ferber. I'm sure his method works and in some cases is appropriate and even necessary. However, I do want to smack some of Dr. Ferber's more extremist followers. These Cry-It-Out Commandos are like drill sergeants in their approach to getting other mothers to follow Ferber's advice—often encouraging new moms to ignore their own instincts.

Once, when I had completely run out of activities to do with my baby, I checked out a local Mommy & Me class to see if it was better than the one I already went to. Because I wasn't an official paying member of the group, I sat back and watched the other mothers interact. One mom, cradling the sweetest, smallest three-month-old baby on her lap, spoke up, complaining that her baby *still* wasn't sleeping through the night. From what I gathered, this woman was having a problem and had been given some advice from the alpha mom in the group the week before. Apparently it wasn't working. "She keeps waking up at four a.m., wanting to be fed!" the frazzled mom continued, barely meeting anyone's gaze.

"You have to be tough with her," Alpha scolded in classic Cry-It-Out Commando style. "Turn off the monitor, put on some headphones, and have a martini or call one of us, but whatever you do, do not go into her room. It won't work if you're not committed!"

It was immediately clear that this whole "just watching" thing wasn't working out for me. "What time is your baby going to bed?" I asked quietly.

"Six," she answered, not seeing where I was going with this. I semiquickly did the math. Her baby was sleeping ten hours straight! That baby, who very easily could've been a preemie, was going ten hours without complaint. I felt myself getting agitated.

"You cannot cave!" scolded Alpha, who was now at the top of my shit-list. "Thanks to Dr. Ferber my baby's been sleeping through the night since he was four weeks old."

Four weeks old? A four-week-old only stops screaming because they've come to the painful realization that no one's ever coming to get them. In my book that's not an accomplishment, that's a felony. What was wrong with this woman?

"But I really feel like she's crying because she's hungry!" Frazzled Mom explained.

I was practically lactating just listening to this, and I hadn't breast-fed in months. I couldn't keep quiet another millisecond. "Then you need to feed your baby!" I said, with way more force than originally intended.

"But they're saying I can't." She gestured feebly toward Alpha Mom and a couple of her cronies, who promptly looked away.

Alpha stared me down. She was a petite Jewish woman with bad highlights and a worse boob job. I felt confident I could take her in a fight.

"They're not your baby's mother," I announced. "You are. You are the one listening to her cry. You know your baby and can figure out what she needs." The room went silent, and I had a sneaking suspicion I wouldn't be welcomed back. It was kind of freeing really, so I kept going. "Your baby's sleeping ten hours straight and she's only three months old. If after ten hours she's crying inconsolably, you probably need to feed her."

Of course, Alpha wasn't going down that easily. "Dr. Ferber says it's all about getting the baby on the mother's schedule so everyone will be happier. She shouldn't have to get up at four in the morning. The baby needs to learn."

She'd won my vote for Selfish Mother of the Year, and I was on a roll. "I haven't read Dr. Ferber's book cover to cover, but obviously you haven't read it at all, because he doesn't suggest using this method on a hungry three-month-old. In fact, Ferber doesn't suggest using it on a baby under six months. Not only that but he doesn't advocate not going in to check on and comfort your baby. And I think that any sleep method is supposed to be used for the health of the child and not just for the convenience of the parent."

Screw it, the Mommy & Me group was a hundred and fifty bucks I didn't need to spend anyway.

I walked to the parking lot alone, but another mother approached me as I was getting my daughter strapped into the car. "I'm so glad you said something," she whispered. "No one wants to stand up to that woman. Especially me, I'm horrible with confrontation."

How lucky for me that I don't have that issue.

As far as my own baby's sleeping habits, my husband and I tried a little of everything. We let her cry for a little bit, we stuck to bedtime routines, and we also made an unsuccessful attempt to reintroduce swaddling, after watching the DVD *The Happiest Baby on the Block*. This is where, with the baby's arms by their sides, you wrap the baby up like a burrito so they don't wake up by accidentally hitting themselves in the face. The DVD claims all babies love it even if they protest. After the first eight weeks our baby wasn't merely protesting, she was rioting. We tried it again, but she could escape from the tightest swaddle quicker than Houdini out of a straitjacket.

We started putting the baby down awake in her bassinet, which we pimped out by putting a firm pillow underneath the so-called padding that it came with. (Yes, I know the SIDS police would put out a warrant for my arrest if they heard about it.) Finally I had to surrender. Surrender to the fact that she was going to do things such as sleeping through the night on her own schedule, and all I could do was try to start her off with some good habits and up my coffee intake by about sixteen cups.

Eventually one of those things must've started working, or she straightened herself out and started falling asleep at nine thirty. Then at nine, then eight thirty . . . then she started teething and it all went to shit.

Remember, there are as many different ideas for getting your baby to sleep as there are babies, but there is no one *right* way to get your baby to sleep. I suggest you steer clear of anyone who claims otherwise. There is only what works for you and what you feel comfortable with. Short of slipping your kid a Unisom, there's not much you can do but wait it out.

All I can say is what another mother said to me when I was crying to her at one a.m. When things seem really tough, try to remember your baby will not be doing this when they're eighteen. Okay, they *will*, but you won't have to stay up with them. Then again, you still won't be able to sleep, wondering if they'll bring your car home in one piece.

The Feeding Frenzy

If you're like most new parents, one of the biggie mile-stones you will be looking forward to in your baby's early days is giving him his first taste of solid food. For the initial few months of life babies subsist solely on a liquid diet—much like they will in college. But after about four to six months you will finally get the go ahead to serve up a real meal. As keyed up as you prob-ably are, I feel it's up to me to warn you it's bound to be a little anticlimactic. Not to mention what no one tells you: Baby food is expensive, the cleanup is a bitch, and there are people who have *way* too many opinions about this issue.

There is little variation in how most people go about starting solid foods. It's fairly boring. Your pediatrician will probably advise you to start off by offering a single grain cereal, like oatmeal. I was really fired up to give my baby her first taste of solid food. I figured if she was any-thing like me, she wouldn't be able to shovel it in fast enough. But the second the spoon hit her mouth, she promptly spit it out like a wine connoisseur who'd accidentally taken a swig of Bartles and Jaymes. I couldn't believe it, it was like she was slapping food in the face.

I said to her, "Listen, little missy, I will not have you dissing the very thing that's brought me so much comfort over the years and gotten me through many a tough time. Food's been my constant companion through temp jobs, insomnia, depression, and Internet dating. You don't know food well enough to reject it yet. I know oatmeal ain't exactly a Happy Meal, but we don't start with that right out of the gate. Give it time."

It does take babies a little while to understand that food is their friend. And for some of us, our best friend.

Once your baby's been lukewarm on cereal for a week or so, you're free to move on to fruits, veggies, and eventually liquid meats, introducing the foods one at a time and waiting three or four days between each new food to be sure your baby doesn't have an allergic reaction. Some doctors will tell you to give fruit last, because they worry that once a baby gets a taste of sweet fruit they'll lose all interest in anything nutritious like vegetables. As if fruit were some sort of gateway drug that would lead to the harder stuff . . . like Nilla Wafers.

Some other doctors advise color coordinating foods—orange foods first, such as sweet potatoes and carrots, then moving on to greens and so on. I have to draw the line at this approach. It's not a home improvement project; it's lunch. But maybe this approach works better for people who are great at accessorizing.

Once your baby is eating an array of jarred food, *especially* the orange-colored variety, prepare yourself for your entire kitchen to look like a Jackson Pollock exhibit. There will be food on the walls, the floor, the couch, your next-door neighbor's couch—no matter what you do, your baby is going to get it everywhere. "Wait, what about bibs?" you ask. Ha! Using a bib on your baby while they're eating is like trying to catch a tidal wave with a sponge. If you are going to use bibs, I'd recommend the disposable ones. Otherwise you will spend most of your daylight hours doing laundry. Your best bet is to feed the baby completely naked near a fire station, so you can have a powerful hose at your disposal, or do what I do and go a few weeks between feedings to get your house back in order.

However you go about it, eventually your baby will have chowed her way through all the different first foods, and will be ready to move on to more adventurous fare. This is the first juncture where new mothers are left to their own terrified discretion, and it's around this time that food paranoia seems to set in for a lot of women. It's easy to get overly concerned with what, when, and how much your baby can eat. But beware: Insecurity can leave you vulnerable to the food fanatics.

While out to lunch with a couple of other new mothers, I gave my ten-month-old baby some Chiclets-size bites of my grilled salmon. Well, you would've thought I'd added Drano to her sippy cup, the way one of the women looked at me.

"What's wrong?" I asked.

"You should never give a baby fish at her age!"

"Oh, really. Why not?"

"Why not? Well, for one thing she could be allergic or get salmonella. Unless you're back there in the kitchen, you don't know if it's clean or how they prepare it. Plus, don't you know that fish is loaded with mercury and . . . other diseases?"

I considered her point for about three seconds. "What do you think babies eat in Japan?"

Aah, sweet silence.

Think about it; there are millions of little babies eating sushi for dinner every night and doing fine. And they're probably not appreciating it, exactly like babies with their oatmeal here.

"And what about all the babies in Italy eating pepperoni pizza, or the ones in France drinking champagne and smoking cigarettes?" At this point I felt I was stating the obvious.

Yes, parents all around the world feed their babies all kinds of food, and the mommy police don't try to have them arrested.

It was then I decided to rescind my kind offer of salmon to my baby—not because it's not healthy for her, which it is—but she wasn't going to appreciate my fourteen-dollar grilled fish nearly as much as I was, anyway!

There are no hard-set rules. Even when it seems like there are rules, they can sometimes be broken.

For instance, the boxes of baby cookies, crackers, and finger foods tell you your baby isn't ready to eat them unless she's "chest off the floor and crawling," as the label explains.

Being food-paranoid myself for the first couple months of feeding her, I'd avoided these snacks. But after seeing another woman's baby enjoying a little cereal cookie, I bummed one off her and tried giving it to my baby. She loved it. Of course, I was a little anxious because I knew she wasn't *officially* "chest off the floor." But as I watched her happily gumming the cookie into a fine paste, I had an epiphany: The cookie makers probably tell you your baby has to be off the floor so that your baby won't lie on his back while eating, possibly choking and making the company liable in a big, fat, nasty lawsuit. *But* if you're smart enough to realize that your baby must be watched like a hawk when he puts anything in his mouth, or if, like me, you find watching your baby eating more exciting than seeing someone fall in a figure skating championship, then you can go ahead and give your kid those treats ahead of the box's schedule.

Yes, there are some foods that should be avoided until babies are at least six months to a year old. Those foods include peanuts, honey, strawberries, citrus fruits, chocolate, and egg yolks, because of possible allergic reactions, but other than that, when it comes to nourishing your baby, you need to lighten up and use common sense.

But this doesn't stop women from trying to control everything their babies eat. For some women this food obsession bypasses the type of food and goes straight to texture. This type of woman wants all food to be as smooth as Kojak's head, and they refuse to put anything past their baby's lips that has not been pureed to within an inch of its life. Seriously, this woman will put pudding in a blender.

Oh, and beware of the "make all my own baby food" mommies. These women will do anything to try to suck you into their web. My feeling is, a lot of people build their own houses too, but that doesn't mean we all need to break out overalls and blueprints.

Some of these extremists will try to scare you into joining them by insisting that homemade food is so much healthier. "This way, I know exactly what goes into every single thing I give my baby." Implying what—that by not making your own food you'd just as soon feed your kid a tin can for dessert? Well, if you're the type who likes making all your baby food, you're probably also the type of person who's into making your own Christmas wreaths and thinks tofu is a meal. I've napped through more than one lecture on making homemade, pureed, slow-cooked chicken that will take you two hours to make and your baby two seconds to smear on the high chair. That sounds like a real blast.

Some women actually think of making baby food as an entertaining diversion. A mommy once invited me to take a *class* on how to make your own baby food. Oh yeah, that's how I want to spend my Saturday night, learning how to make dishes like banana peach compote, recipes that are way more elaborate than anything you would ever make for yourself. For a hundred bucks you can learn to make a three-course fresh-food meal for your baby—the operative word being "you." Yeah, *you* can learn. The day I make a three-course meal for my child is the day she learns to bus her own table and leave a generous tip. Until then I have some Gerber pureed pears she may be interested in.

Don't get me wrong, it's not like I'm some kind of jarred-food activist. I'm all for giving your baby wholesome fresh foods when you can. But . . . here comes some startling news, you probably have some healthy food for your baby right in your very own refrigerator. Let's all slow down and take a moment with that one. I'm all about cutting up pea-size pieces of cheese with a fresh fruit garnish. Steaming your own vegetables seems like a great idea too. I've never done it, but it sounds terrific. But there are limits. Let's not push it.

I'm sure organic foods are fantastic too. There's certainly no argument to be made against organic food, if you can afford it. But if you choose to feed your baby organics, it doesn't mean your child now has "special needs." If you are generously invited to come with your two toddlers to stay at an old college friend's house for a couple of days, you shouldn't e-mail that friend a few days before your arrival a shopping list of organic foods and juices that your friend absolutely must stock up on. If you really feel that those are the only foods your precious children should be eating, then for God's sake bring your own. Otherwise you may find that not only has your invite been revoked, but you have been blocked from ever sending another e-mail. But what do I know?

Some women are also consumed by how much their baby consumes. Babies will eat until they're full. You should never try to regulate how much your baby eats unless your pediatrician tells you otherwise, or you're trying to get her into baby modeling. Then, obviously, you don't want her to be a fatty. But don't put your baby on Atkins, because babies get extra fussy when you restrict their carbs. You might want to try the South Beach Diet, and if that doesn't work, think positive, there's always plus-size baby modeling.

Hey, in my parents' day they couldn't start feeding us nonorganic, non-allergy-proof food fast enough. Doctors told women to start their babies on cereal at about nineteen days, move to fruits at four weeks, and begin tuna casserole as soon as they saw fit. Sure we may be appalled at that notion now, yet we seem to be okay.

Okay, technically a lot of us are logging serious hours on the therapist's couch, but I think that has little to do with the baby-food situation. And, then again, a few of us are just fine.

Bon appétit.

Baby on Bored

If you've read your share of baby books—and you're reading this one, so I'm going out on a limb to say you have—you're probably under the impression that your baby needs more stimulation than a Jack Russell terrier. And shortly after you pass your placenta you will undoubtedly start trying to think of ways to constantly entertain your child. You will go from a sex goddess to a low-rent circus of games, funny faces, baby talk, and other things that make you a hero to your baby and completely asexual to your husband and the rest of the world.

For the first few weeks it's all you can do to feed, diaper, and soothe—a seemingly endless cycle of lather, rinse, repeat that leaves you exhausted. During this time almost anything can be background noise. Yes, you can watch HBO to your heart's content while your baby is nursing (a bottle or a boob) or sleeping. You may think this period is rough, but trust me, you will look back at this time as your last glorious weeks of freedom.

Way too soon your baby will leave the sleeping-sixteen-hours-a-day state and all of a sudden you will find him looking at you like, "Now what?" And you'll be like, "What do you mean, 'Now what?' Don't you want to sleep through *The Sopranos* like always?" But as you watch Tony and his buddies off another fringe character while your baby lies there wide awake absently monitoring the screen, you will get the sneaking suspicion that your baby's bored. As you look at her tiny face, you may wonder, "What the hell are you thinking about, lying there staring at the ceiling?" And then you'll think, "Great. Now there's two people who I will have to wonder what the hell they're thinking."

I know for me, I like to have my mind occupied at all times. I enjoy reading the Internet or watching TV or talking on the phone or reading a magazine or doing all four at once. Nothing makes me crazier than sitting still. I'm type A. I once succumbed to peer pressure and tried yoga, but I found it as relaxing as a tax audit. I think I'm the only person whose blood pressure actually went up doing Downward Facing Dog. So of course I frequently worried that my baby was bored.

Even if you're mellow and easygoing, you're going to want to stimulate your baby, and you will do it naturally by singing and talking and paying focused attention. But you may secretly wonder if you are ever really doing enough.

Other go-getter mommies will only further your

fears when you see how much dedicated attention they're giving to stimulating their babies. These women are not your friends.

I fell victim to someone like this. I'll call her . . . Angie, because that's her actual name. Angie e-mailed me and, I'm guessing, a hundred of her closest friends an online photo album containing snapshots of her four-month-old baby. Now, normally I would've reported it as spam, but at the time I too had a newborn. So out of lingering postpartum sentimentality and sheer boredom, I made the mistake of opening it and browsing through the pictures. I was confronted with dozens of photos of her darling baby posed in all different situations, with cute little captions like, "Baby's Night Out" and "Emma Cruisin' with Her Best Friend, Mikayla." Best friend? Wow, I don't even have a best friend, which I blame on never having joined a sorority.

I have to be honest. I was thrown off my game. I started thinking, *Am I a bad mom? My baby isn't doing half the stuff this baby is doing. This baby's on the go! She's going for nature walks in the park, having social outings to the movies, taking guided museum tours, and to top it all off this bee-yotch has a best friend!* I felt so bad for my own baby that I decided I better report myself to child services. But then I had a shot of Jägermeister—okay two—and got a grip on myself. BEST FRIEND? Wait a minute. Hold the phone. Babies don't have best friends! At four months old, babies don't even know that's their own foot they're playing with.

Then I took an even closer look. Not one outfit change going on in any of the pictures. Either Angie didn't have a very lucrative baby shower or all these activities happened in one day. One day and fifty photo ops! Suddenly it dawned on me, my baby had plenty going on. It was Angie who needed a hobby.

But just in case, I thought I'd check it out with my pediatrician. "Should I be stimulating my baby more?" I asked on my next visit (the "more" was added for me). My levelheaded doctor merely looked at me. "Your baby is stimulated by everything she sees and hears. She doesn't need you to buy special things for her. Right now everything is new."

What a relief. I hadn't thought of it that way, but it made perfect sense. Seeing a tree is a big day for an eight-week-old. To a baby, looking at a stop sign is like mental Pilates. "Whoa, a stop sign! Red! And not evenly shaped! Whew, I need to chill out for a few minutes. Catch my breath. Maybe take a really quick nap."

The baby books will overwhelm you with all kinds of stimulating activities to try with your baby. They suggest that your baby will love peekaboo, blowing bubbles, looking at paintings on the wall, horsey rides on your knee, seeing baby's face in the mirror, looking at a display of family photos, holding a shiny object on a string and waving it, pat-a-cake, rolling a ball, tickle-me-till-I-stop-breathing, taking a tour of your friend's medicine cabinet, etc., etc., etc.

Yes, your baby will love all these things, but obviously you cannot do these things all day long, otherwise you will suffer from baby stimulation burnout. Peekaboo is, admittedly, a good time to be had by all, but after about twenty minutes you will long for the excitement of cleaning out your shower drain. The same goes for pat-a-cake; it's fun but, let's be honest, not eating-a-bagel-and-cream-cheese fun.

Well, here's the good news. We don't need to be torturing ourselves. The books aren't suggesting you spend *all day* trying to stimulate the baby. These activities are meant as helpful hints for those times when you are gazing into your baby's eyes and wondering, "What the hell do you want to do now?" and your baby is looking back at you like, "Whatever you want to do," and you are looking back saying, "No, I'm asking you. What do you want to do?" And your baby falls asleep, and you think, "Great, I guess I didn't do anything interesting enough and now his little mind is atrophying!" Yes, let other moms keep their babies entertained all day long and take pictures of it to their hearts' content. You need to lie on the couch and watch *The Simpsons*.

Now you know that you can sing "Itsy-Bitsy Spider," throw in a couple rounds of "Wheels on the Bus," and take a break. You don't need to entertain your baby like you're on a date. Come on, you don't have that much in common, anyway. Would you purposely hang out with someone whose interests include: pooping, drooling, crying, and yelling shrilly in restaurants twenty-four hours a day? Okay, if they *weren't* a millionaire? No. So why pretend that you love it? Of course you love your baby and you're willing to make sacrifices, but the activities they can join you in at first are limited. So be calm in the knowledge that your baby needs only to be close to you to have a good time. Isn't that sweet? When's the last time your husband said that?

May I Introduce You to . . . Your Babysitter

The first time I left my daughter in the care of someone other than my husband or my mother, she was eleven weeks old. I was not working in an "official" capacity, the kind where people commemorate the end of the work week by giving you money, having chosen to stay home and care for her myself. But I quickly realized that five days a week alone with an infant while my husband was at work was a lot to take on. I figured hiring someone to come over a few hours a week would enable me to get in some much missed quality online poker time, or at least the occasional shower. So I decided to hire a sitter.

But how does one go about finding the right person to care for their child?

The first thing *I* did was send out a mass e-mail to all the women on my neighborhood Yahoo! Internet group. To be honest I didn't know many of them, but I thought, *What the hell, they're all mothers. Someone among them must have a nanny looking to pick up a few extra hours.* I got back a ton of responses—from other women who were also looking for a babysitter and who "would LOVE it" if someone could please refer them to a sitter as well. Fantastic, I'd created more competition for myself. Listen, bitches, write your own mass e-mail! This was going to be harder than I thought. I wondered if at eleven weeks my daughter was old enough to look after herself, but I figured she needed at least a couple more days. She was a little immature for her age.

Next I tried asking a few random people for names of potential caregivers. This technique is a little tricky. You don't necessarily want to ask people whom *they* use, because it's not the same as asking them who waxes their eyebrows. It can smell an awful lot like poaching, and that can make a mom a bit testy. Okay, testier than they already are. You need to take a subtler tack and simply ask if they can recommend someone. This worked a bit better for me. I got one name from a woman I schmoozed briefly at the park. Then the realtor who sold me my house referred me to her backup babysitter. A good friend recommended her new roommate, who had been working as a nanny. Plus, a neighbor came through with her full-time nanny's eighteen-year-old daughter. I set up all four interviews for one day.

I had a bunch of questions ready to ask. Like, number one: Do you smoke? And if so, can I bum a cigarette? (I was a little nervous.) And then there's the classic, Where do you see yourself in six weeks? But I quickly realized how absurd that was. I wasn't going to find out if someone was reliable and trustworthy by asking lame job interview questions—as if *I'd* ever been honest in a job interview.

No, it made more sense to chat them up and try to get a sense of their vibe. I knew if I didn't want to invest in a nanny-cam, I'd have to read between the lines for signs of a great or lousy babysitter. Did she seem comfortable with a new baby? Did she have her own transportation? Did she have track marks? But after talking to each girl at length, I thought they all seemed really sweet and relaxed with my baby, so in the end I went with my gut and picked the one with the loosest schedule. My gut came through like a champ. We still have the same babysitter, and at this point she's almost like an overpaid member of our family.

I'd say the only drawback is sometimes I actually worry that my child likes our babysitter a little *too* much. Once in a while when my daughter pulls away from me and reaches her little chubby arms out to "not me," I find it necessary to have a little heart-to-heart and straighten her out. "Hey, kid, who's the one who breast-fed you for three weeks? Not her! Yeah, I know she's blond and young and nice, but *I'm* the one who's going to put you through law school! Me!" And then I pull out my trump card and show her my C-sec scar. I think she gets the message.

But the freedom that comes with a babysitter is well worth the occasionally damaged pride. You may not believe it, but there are actually people out there who have never experienced the sheer joy of having someone that's not them put their baby to bed. If you're one of those people, take heed: If by the time your precious infant is an aware and opinionated toddler you have never left the house without him, this is going to come back and bite you in the ass. Your child will become quite accustomed to being put to bed only by mommy. Eventually you'll have a tiny tyrant on your hands who will outright refuse to be put to bed by anyone but you, and there will be hours of screaming and hell to pay.

I know a woman who felt so bad leaving her baby with a sitter that she never did, and now it's impossible because she has a controlling six-year-old whom she has to lie next to, rubbing his back for an hour and a half every night until he dozes off to sleep. This is no way to live! If anyone's in need of a damn massage after a long day of child care it's her!

If you're having a tough time loosening your grasp, you need to realize that this is a valid fear, but one that has gone too far and needs to be nipped in the bud—stat, before it gets even more out of hand. Usually it's not your child who has separation anxiety; it's you.

Try treating it like a phobia. Look, if people can suffer from arachibutyrophobia, which is the fear of peanut butter sticking to the roof of the mouth, then I have no doubt there's a clinical name for being afraid to leave your baby with a sitter for a half hour while you run to 7-Eleven.

One way to go is exposure therapy, where you submit yourself to the situation that causes anxiety or panic. You then learn to "ride out" the distress until the anxiety passes, gradually increasing the duration of exposure with each session until you can tolerate the situation without hyperventilating. That's exactly how I learned to sit through an entire episode of *According to Jim*.

First try leaving the room for a few seconds—*without* your baby. Once you're in another room, you need to get your mind off your child. Do some deep breathing exercises, count to ten, picture Christian Bale in a pair of boxer briefs. Now go back in and look at the baby. See? Everything's fine. He's just poking stuff into an unprotected electrical outlet. Once you feel comfortable with that, keep extending the time until you get to the point where you can microwave an entire Lean Cuisine while your child plays by his- or herself. Before you know it, you will be ready to leave your baby with the nice girl with the tongue piercing at Jamba Juice "only for a few minutes while I try on a pair of jeans at the boutique next door."

It's natural to feel anxious when you first leave your baby in someone else's care. But believe me, it's necessary. Do yourself a favor and hire a babysitter while your baby is young and they don't know anything different. It will save you years of aggravation.

But please don't call mine. She's not available.

Nanny Nurturing

So you've managed to snag yourself a babysitter whom you and your children adore, someone who takes the care of your children seriously yet knows how to show them a good time. Consider yourself lucky. Now it's your job to ensure she sticks around. A good babysitter, someone you trust, is a valuable commodity. Be careful, other women are going to want to steal her.

It's imperative that you learn how to properly treat and care for your babysitter, because if you mistreat one, it's sure to become a huge problem. Pissing off a babysitter is a lot like pissing off the mob—word will spread and you will find it next to impossible to get anyone to work for you. Need a babysitter for a Saturday night . . . fuhgeddaboudit! You better be stocked up on Disney classics and finger paints, because it's gonna be a long year of one-on-one quality time with your child.

It doesn't have to go down like that. All it takes is a bit of awareness and a shred of human decency. Here are a few tips to make sure you don't accidentally ruin your reputation in the Nanny Network.

When your sitter comes over, don't shove your baby into her arms the second she walks through the door, saying, "You're just in time to change a poopy diaper!" or "Thank God you're here! It's time to give Ellie her lunch." Let your sitter put her stuff down and maybe get settled a moment. Think about it; when you go to work, do you start the second your butt hits the chair? No. You check your e-mail, grab a cup of coffee, and find out if your coworker slept with that guy she went out with the night before. And if she did sleep with him, you know nothing's getting done until after lunch. Give your babysitter the same courtesy. Before handing over the baby, ask her who she slept with the night before.

Your babysitter does not run on smiles. You need to supply her with something to eat while she's at your house. Be considerate of her. You probably have about eighteen different menu choices for your kid but haven't given a single thought to what your sitter will eat on her eight-hour shift. She doesn't want to dig through your refrigerator, trying to figure out how long the leftover pad Thai's been in there. And she probably doesn't want to eat anything with the label GERBER on it. Be a sport, buy her a salad.

I know it's uncomfortable, but next we need to discuss money. If you are paying your babysitter an hourly amount, and she stays for another portion of an hour, for the love of all things holy, when you go to write the check, *round up*. If there's one thing a babysitter won't welcome, it's the use of a decimal point. If you feel you must write a check for $76, go ahead, but don't under any circumstance write it for $75.60. Ever.

Along these same lines, when you pay your baby-sitter, pay for *all* the hours she was there. Don't write the check out while you're leaving the restaurant. You need to include the forty-five minutes you spent digging around for your checkbook after you got home. She's not tossing you a freebie hour. And don't make her mention it, because she won't. She'll simply become "open to other offers." How do you think I snagged mine?

Please don't kill the messenger. I'm only trying to help you here.

Do not ever dock your babysitter's pay for being a few minutes late. You are entrusting them with your most precious cargo, your child! The last thing you want is a resentful babysitter. When you piss off a waitress, she might put Visine in your Diet Coke. You don't want a babysitter doing the equivalent with your children.

If you are expecting someone to clean your house as well as watch the kiddies, you need to be perfectly clear when you are offering the job and you need to compensate them accordingly. Anything beyond fixing a meal for the kids and cleaning up after them is considered housekeeping and is a separate job. Yes, throwing in a couple of loads of laundry is considered housekeeping.

Sorry. I know it might make you feel weird that while your baby is napping the day away, your sitter is kicking it on the couch, reading the latest Oprah book club offering, but this isn't Burger King and there's no "time to lean, time to clean" policy in effect. Hey, at least she got your baby to sleep. A well-rested baby is a better behaved baby after she leaves.

One more thing. If your kid is ill, stay home if at all possible. Your child will feel much safer and more comfortable with you home, and your babysitter will be pleased about not being projectile-vomited on all day long. If it's not an option for you to stay home, at least have the courtesy to tell your babysitter the situation up front. Surprising them with your sick kid will get you kicked off the Most Wanted Babysitting Gigs list, pronto.

Many moms tend to forget the teeny detail that their babysitter is being paid to do a job. Instead they're convinced that the babysitter loves their kids as much as they do and would happily sing "Itsy-Bitsy Spider" eighteen times a day just for the *privilege* of spending time with such adorable kids. I'm sure your babysitter is fond of your kids, but this is a *job*, and I bet she'd also be fond of a dollar more an hour somewhere else.

I'm sorry to be the one to break it to you, but even if your babysitter loves your kid, she doesn't love them as much as you do. And if she does love them as much as you do—be very, very careful. She may have a serious mental disorder and could be plotting to steal your family away by seducing your husband into an affair, murdering you, and becoming the perfect mother to your child. If you haven't seen *The Hand That Rocks the Cradle*, rent it right now, and then give your babysitter a raise.

Other Types of Child Care

Day care—This is a place outside of your home where you leave your children to be cared for. This is a great place for your child to make new friends, do fun activities, and pick up a raging case of scabies.

The twelve-year-old down the street—The good news is, they'll probably work for cheap. The bad news is, if I wanted someone to turn on MTV for two hours while the baby is parked next to them chewing on a dirty sock, I could hire myself.

Au pair—I don't speak French, but I'm pretty sure "au pair" loosely translates to "hostage." These poor girls come from another country and watch your children in exchange for room and board. And how do you repay them? By giving them a curfew, which quickly becomes the only thing standing between them and the life they came out here to lead.

Nanny—A nanny is a woman you hire to watch your kid in your home full-time while you go to work, or it's someone a celebrity hires full-time "just because."

Grandparents—If they're around, your parents can take care of your kids. Although you may not have to pay in the monetary sense, you will pay. Oh yes, *you will pay*.

Advice: The Good, the Bad, and the Ugly

I would like to know why it is that I've paid therapists upward of a hundred and fifty dollars an hour to give me advice and they will not do it. Even if you ask them straight-out, "What should I do?" they will look at you blandly and say, "What do *you* think you should do?" And then they will glance not so subtly over your head at the clock that's positioned there for just that reason, and say, "Well, our time is up for today. But I will see you next week and continue to let you make the same mistakes and repeat the same patterns while *I* continue to collect your money." It's maddening. Therapists refuse to tell you what to do, even though they're both qualified and paid to do it!

Yet when you have a baby, people who are completely unqualified, people at least ten years short of any sort of medical degree, will have *a lot* to say about your parenting choices.

Starting when you're pregnant, people will have no problem flashing you the hairy eyeball if you so much as sniff a piece of brie or munch an itty-bitty spicy tuna roll. And once you pass that placenta, people will charge out of the woodwork to give you advice. Free of charge. Suddenly everyone's an expert on child rearing—from the lady who does your bikini wax to your postman. Criminals will voluntarily leave witness protection in order to tell you *not* to start your baby on solids until they're at least six months old, for fear of potential allergies. Oh yeah, people love to give advice! There should be a twelve-step program for it, because for some people it's a high.

While some advice is actually helpful, mostly you're going to find that the world is full of bitchy hall monitors who are just waiting to catch you doing something wrong. "You shouldn't ever let a baby watch television until they're at least fourteen years old or they'll surely develop ADD." "Don't let your baby use an ExerSaucer. My pediatrician warned me that they can ruin your baby's posture and affect their walking." How many people have you met with walking problems caused by ExerSaucer use? "Oh, this limp? Old ExerSaucer injury." Exactly, hardly any.

I once found myself stopped at a red light in my ultrasafe and sturdy Volvo equipped with six—count 'em, six—airbags, with my baby strapped in her rear-facing Graco deluxe infant seat (okay, I'm not 100 percent sure it's a deluxe, but it was the fanciest one you could buy for less than two hundred dollars), with fire-station approved installation. Suddenly a woman in an SUV pulls up next to me on the passenger side and starts honking. I look over at her and she's frantically pointing to my backseat and gesturing wildly. I couldn't understand her, so naturally I imagined the worst; my baby was slumped over in her little seat, having strangled herself on the restraining straps. I assumed the real reason I was enjoying some peace and quiet was not because I'd succeeded in getting her to doze off with the help of a Norah Jones CD, but because she was UNCONSCIOUS. I silently cursed myself for not having taken an infant CPR refresher course in the last few hours.

Leaning over as fast as I could, I powered both windows down on the passenger side and strained to hear my next-door car neighbor. Hands staying on her steering wheel, she tilted her head out the window, highlighted ponytail flapping in the breeze, and yelled, "You're supposed to put the handle on the car seat *all the way up.*"

"Huh?" I strained to understand what *had to be an emergency* for her to be practically stroking out.

"The handle of the baby seat! That's a safety hazard. It's supposed to be over your baby's head!!"

"It is."

"No. ALL THE WAY UP." I had no idea what she was even talking about. But whatever she was concerned about was not a safety hazard. "Don't worry," the aging cheerleader said. "Someone had to point it out to me, too."

I yelled back, "Listen, psycho, if I'd left my car seat on the roof of my car with my baby still in it, by all means let me know. Short of that, mind your own damn business," which I'm sure would've taught her a lesson if she hadn't already powered up her window. And with that she sped off.

I was in shock. I'd just been the victim of a drive-by scolding.

"That's nothing," a friend of mine said when I told her how mad I was. "Did I tell you about getting pulled over by the Sunscreen Police?" Apparently she was out walking her ten-month-old baby boy when an elderly neighbor she didn't know came running (I use the term "running" very loosely in this case) out of her house and down her front walk, stopping directly in my friend's path. "Hello, Mommy," Sunscreen Lady said sternly. "I hope you put sunscreen on your little man." My friend laughed nervously and said, "Actually, no. I'm a bad mommy and I forgot," which, in my mind, was a huge mistake. Admitting an error to these kinds of people is like parading the mailman in front of your dog. The old lady cried, "Aha! Well, then, you're not going anywhere. You are going to turn around and march back home to get some protection." My friend actually felt guilty.

Strangers are certainly not the only people who can make you homicidal with their unsolicited advice. Grandparents and in-laws do it too, and they're harder to avoid since you need them for last-minute babysitting.

One problem with the older generation's advice is that anything you do for your baby short of giving them up for adoption will be considered spoiling them. "You're holding your baby? Again? Hmmm . . . interesting. I'm surprised he can play by himself on the floor for five minutes, since he's being handled all the time."

Anything you do to your baby that they didn't do to you will be deemed completely unnecessary and will be met with a rolling of the eyes. "So, let me get this straight, you're putting her in the infant seat *and* you're strapping her in? That seems like overkill. In my day we didn't have *infant seats*. We held the babies in our laps and took out extra car insurance."

Also be warned, grandparents are appalled at the notion of a baby sleeping in your bed with you, even if it's only for a few nights. "You're putting her in the bed with you? She's going to get used to that and you'll never be able to get her to sleep in her own bed. You know you slept in your own crib clear on the other side of the country from the very first night home from the hospital. And we didn't have monitors back then either! We used a tin can with a piece of string."

Really. And now I can't go to sleep without polishing off half a bottle of wine. Coincidence?

On the flip side grandparents can be the source of some truly great advice—advice that is very relaxing, mainly because they were raised in a time when people weren't losing their shit over every little thing they read on the Internet. Yeah, they had no Internet! If they wanted porn, they had to make their own! There's something to be said for the fact that their kids sur-vived formula feeding, drinking straight from the gar-den hose, removing toast from the toaster with a fork, and going trick-or-treating by themselves in question-able neighborhoods. Of course, this was back when parents thought Father Bill's showering with the boys after the church basketball game was *all about hygiene*.

There's no getting around the fact that as a new par-ent, you will be subjected to an awful lot of strong opin-ions about how you should or shouldn't raise your child. For some people this will be a load off—those passive souls who love nothing more than to be told what to do, the folks who consult their horoscope before deciding whether or not to have pancakes for breakfast, and the ones who check with seventeen friends before switching moisturizers. Some other people can be given advice all day long and they're immune to it. You can recognize these folks by their HOW AM I RAISING MY KID? DIAL 1-800-EAT SHIT bumper stickers. But for a lot of us anxious types, unsolicited advice is like the Muzak version of "Girl from Ipanema." We didn't ask to hear it, but now that we have, we won't be able to get it out of our heads. If you fall into this group, you have my sympathy, but unfortunately, I can't advise you on what to do. Don't worry, though, there are a lot of people who can and will.

Remember, if you're a mother, you are being told

how to do your *job*. If those advice-givers are going to critique you, they better be open to a little constructive criticism themselves. Next time your postman tells you the best way to get your baby to sleep, try telling him, "You might want to hold the 'Photos: Don't Bend' packages *flat*" or "Is there any way you could drop off our mail sometime before *midnight?*" That might change his tune. But probably not.

Developmental Breakdown

It seems quaint to recall that once upon a time babies were allowed to grow and develop at their own pace, free of benchmarks, percentile groups, and the nervous eyes of competitive adults. Maybe it was because most parents of the era were too busy trying to scratch out a living from the barren family farm to give a damn, but still, for the babies the first couple years were basically a free ride.

Now the grace period is up by the time they get to the hospital nursery, when the newborn is tossed into the developmental Olympics. On arrival they're given the Apgar test and scored on Activity (Muscle Tone), Pulse, Grimace (Reflex Irritability), Appearance (Skin Color), and Respiration, and we're off and running from there—measuring our babies against other babies.

We all need to do our part to keep this in check before it spreads like strep to all the mommies. Of course you're going to be proud of your baby's developmental accomplishments. There will be much excitement in your home the first time your baby crawls or waves bye-bye or sits up. But keep in mind that your baby *sat up*—he didn't discover a renewable energy source or land his own show on Nickelodeon. We've turned each natural act of growing into another way to show off. Like a Juicy Couture diaper bag, your child's age when she first walks is getting worn like a badge. I, for one, don't need this kind of pressure.

It doesn't do anyone any good to constantly check to see how your baby is measuring up to other babies the same age. All babies do things at their own pace. At least that's what a new mother might think until she stumbles across books like *Your Baby Week by Week* and other handy primers that dictate what your baby should be accomplishing every seven days. Even though there is that little disclaimer that says, "This is an approximation and not all babies develop at the exact same rate," it's almost impossible not to get caught up in the hysteria.

Anyone prone to excess worry or competitiveness, and good luck finding a mom who isn't overcome by one of these emotions from time to time, can be traumatized by the developmental pressure. I had to toss my milestone book, because it prompted way too many calls to the pediatrician and endless nights on the Internet trying to sleuth out what was wrong with my daughter when she was nine days late in discovering her feet.

Whenever you're somewhere that mommies congregate, one of the first things a woman with a similarly aged baby will ask you is, "Is she doing such and such?" For some it genuinely is a friendly question, meant to break the ice. But in almost any assemblage of mommies there will lurk Competitive Mom. With this woman almost any question of this sort is actually the opening shot in a gunfight at the development corral. And you'd better know that the woman who shelled out eight hundred dollars for that top-shelf stroller is going to be equally invested in making sure her Brianna is the first in the playgroup to drink from a sippy cup. Thus begins a vicious cycle from which no baby will emerge unscathed: The competitive mom will open the competition by asking about something your baby is able to do, and then to top you she'll come up with something your baby can't do but hers is doing fantastically.

I can't tell you how many times I'd run into another mother at a coffee place, and before I'd even gotten out my order for a grande nonfat sugar-free vanilla latte, easy foam, I'd get, "How old's your baby? Seven months? Is she crawling yet?"

And I'd say, "No, not yet," and the other mother would give me that little pity smile, as if I'd told her my kid had a learning disability, and then she'd give a little condescending "Don't worry, she'll get there."

I got so sick of it I came up with my own response.

After that, when I got the next "Is she crawling yet?" I'd answer, "No, but she's reading at a third-grade level. Taught herself." Women like this have no sense of humor. They'd stare at me, mouth agape, until I looked at their baby and gave 'em the old, "Don't worry, she'll get there."

But even with my bravado I was still vulnerable to the developmental anxieties. Not smiling soon enough, what could that mean? Doesn't she like me? Will she ever walk? Why isn't she clapping yet? What if she never claps? She needs to get the clapping thing down or they'll think she's rude after puppet shows!

When a good friend called to tell me that her baby, who was the exact same age as mine, was pulling up to a stand while mine was still lying on the floor like a puddle, I reacted as if my friend had won the lottery. (Okay, not the big lotto millions—more like a fifty-dollar scratcher card, but still.) I hate to admit it, but I secretly wasn't that happy for her, and I kind of hoped she was lying. I instantly felt like I'd failed somehow. Why wasn't *my* baby pulling up yet? I assumed it must be something I was doing wrong. And, sure enough, there were people all too happy to validate that fear.

I brought my daughter to a barbecue when she was eleven months old and not yet walking. The place was a madhouse, with approximately thirty-five people in a yard the size of a handicapped bathroom stall. New faces constantly presented themselves at close range to my daughter, who would scrunch up her face in fear. Needless to say, she was a bit overwhelmed. And needless to say, she spent the ninety minutes we were there in my arms or lap. But one pushy grandmother said, "She's not walking?"

I shook my head. "She's getting close but not yet."

She tsk-tsked me! "Well, I can see why. You're spoiling her, carrying her around like that. That's why she's not walking yet. She doesn't have to!"

Let's just say, there weren't enough wine coolers at that party to make me tolerate any further conversation with that woman.

It's true what the books say. All babies are on their own time lines. Maybe your one-year-old isn't thinking about walking because he's figuring out difficult mathematical equations in his little head. Maybe your baby walks at nine months but won't utter a word until she's six.

And maybe your baby does it all. If that's the case, then go ahead and feel good about it, but don't share the news with random people at Starbucks.

It's not a race. If your baby is an early walker, it means that you have to childproof faster. If they're talking early, it means listening to an extra six months of gibberish. Enjoy the quiet while you still can.

Developmental Timetables

3 months

What the books say your baby should be able to do
Recognize your face, laugh, and do mini-push-ups

What your baby is more likely doing
Looking at you as though she can't quite place you, crying, and peeing through fourteen onesies a day

6 months

What the books say your baby should be able to do
Roll in both directions, imitate sounds, possibly sit without support

What your baby is more likely doing
Spitting food, crying in the car seat, peeing through ten onesies a day

12 months

What the books say your baby should be able to do
Express her wants with words and gesture instead of cry

What your baby is more likely doing
Whining and crying when you can't understand her baffling sounds and gestures

2 years

What the books say your baby should be able to do
Walk down stairs, identify colors, and identify body parts on a doll

What your baby is more likely doing
Throwing tantrums in grocery stores, spilling juice on your white couch, pointing out her "vaginey" at dinner parties

20 years

What the books say your "baby" should be able to do
Vote, make her own meals, and pay her own bills

What your "baby" is more likely doing
Living at home "for another year until I figure out what I want to do with my life," eating your food, using her college fund to buy marijuana

Your Postbaby Social Life

"What social life?" you ask. The one you'll be desperate to regain once you can fit into something other than jogging pants and flip-flops.

If this is your first baby, congrats and look out. The change to a woman's social life after having a baby can be a huge shock to her system. You are about to discover it's a strange and scary new world out there. It's a world complete with different cliques, different clothing, different music, and a completely different lingo—a world that's actually a lot like high school, only with less sexual activity. Far less in my case. Of course, postbirth you're probably even more insecure and vulnerable than you felt in high school, and your hormonal mood swings would put any sixteen-year-old to shame. But the good news is, most moms are all way too fat to be cheerleaders now!

Even if you've been waiting your whole life to have a baby, once you enter the sacred halls of "Mommy High," you are likely to feel terribly alone and like you definitely don't belong. So while your baby is a blob and your single friends want nothing to do with you, it is imperative for you to get some other moms in your life. Yes, you're going to have to find new friends with babies.

In the beginning, while you are still postpartum-y, you will be happy to befriend a lamppost. But within a few weeks you'll probably raise your standards to anyone with an infant and a pulse.

No one knows what you're going through like another new mom, and only other moms can answer questions like "How the fuck does this Diaper Genie work?" and "Does a blow job count as cardiovascular exercise?"

You need moms who can give advice in a nonjudgmental way, moms who've been through it, but still remember how confused and scared they felt when their baby was a newborn. You need friendly faces who can tell you, "I know you're going out of your mind, but you can't bring a twelve-day-old baby to Gymboree. Bring the baby over to my house right now, and don't forget a jumbo bag of Baked! Lay's."

These moms are like the new mommy starter kit. Some of them might work out as decent companions, and some may turn out to be complete freaks; it's a crapshoot. Remember, right now the only thing you have in common with these women is a baby and a big ass.

One day I found myself on a walk in the park with a new mom named Fran, whom I'd met at my neighborhood book club. (When you're a brand-new mother, you'll go to extreme measures to meet other women—like attend a book club, a book club where you haven't read the book, or even bought the book for that matter.) This woman happened to share my zip code and have a baby whose age was similar to my daughter's, so we became friendly by default.

You'll find that in the first couple of years it's all about the baby's age. When your baby is a month old, you'll make friends with anyone who has a baby who's from about four hours to about four months. They need to be sharing your experience. By the time your baby is walking around, you can't hang with the brand-new moms, because your kid won't sit quietly in the stroller for walks. That's when you'll be forced to become a park mom (more on that later).

So the conversation with my default friend Fran turned to jobs—or our lack of them. I was an unemployed writer taking some much-needed time off to stay home with my new baby. She had only recently completed graduate school, and confided that she'd been mulling over the idea of going back to work, except for the minor detail that she'd never worked and had no idea what type of job she wanted to do. But seeing as their bank account was in the negative numbers and a collection agency had them on speed-dial, her husband was hoping she'd see her way clear to bringing a little money into the household. To help, he'd come up with the grand idea of her taking a career aptitude test. In a sort of "do what you love and the money will follow"-type bullshit way the test had instructed her to write down her absolute favorite thing to do. After much thought Fran gleefully shared with me that she'd figured out that the thing she absolutely loved doing most, the thing she was put on this Earth to do, was . . . giving tummy kisses to her baby boy. Uh-huh.

Naturally my first thought was, *That can't possibly pay a lot.* Don't get me wrong, I do love nuzzling my baby's midsection for short bursts of time—and by "bursts" I mean five minutes, tops. But "My favorite thing in life"? Whose favorite thing in life is giving tummy kisses to baby boys? Besides Michael Jackson? But then I thought, *Maybe I'm not doing it right. Maybe I'm not getting the total tummy-kissing experience.* Is there a Learning Annex course I could take that would help me unlock the secrets to making twenty minutes of tummy kissing not seem like two hours? And, if not, maybe this woman should teach one. Clearly she knows something about this whole tummy-kissing business that none of us other mothers have figured out.

And my last thought was, *Next time I go on this walk, I'll be packing a flask.*

Another woman, whom I met in the mall when my baby was only a few weeks old, seemed friendly and eager to make lunch plans with me. All I knew about this woman was that she *loved* Celine Dion—not a promising sign, but we both had babies, so I figured I'd try to make it work. That is, until she showed up with her mom. No warning. She brought her mom to lunch with someone she'd never ever hung out with before. Here's a rule of thumb that you

should follow when meeting another mom for a social outing: You're welcome to bring other moms along with
you—as long as the other mom isn't *your* mom. That's
weird. We're not six years old. We want to talk about stuff
without worrying what our mom (or yours) thinks.

Once you get your shit together, you will realize that
a lot of the moms you've been trying to make conversation with are, well, about as exciting as a near beer. I
finally realized that the problem was I had been hanging
out with mommies. Mommies, it seems, really only want
to talk about their babies. Once I got over my initial
baby shock and realized that there are many other topics out there, I decided I was ready to step up my game.
I needed the company of someone who knew what I was
going through and who, like me, wanted to blur it with
alcohol. I needed a fun mom. You too may at some point
need to break out and meet women with whom you
share interests other than your offspring.

A fun mom, once she's through the sleep deprivation
and the anxiety that comes with nurturing a newborn, will
remember she has other things that bring her pleasure, like
nachos and beer. She'll laugh out loud at a Chris Rock special, and in spite of her new "mommy" status she'll probably still wax her bikini line. A fun mom does not think
infant constipation and the best way to take off pregnancy
pounds pass as scintillating conversation—although when
pressed she will tell you that laxatives work great for both.

If you want to stay sane, you should diligently seek

out women who are like-minded, women who enjoy their children but not at the expense of their senses of humor, their husbands, or their careers.

Hunt them down in their natural habitat: Mexican restaurants at happy hour, their beds at three in the afternoon, and Vegas. You'll definitely want to avoid notorious mommy hangouts: Hallmark stores, Color Me Mine, and any children's shops with "Li'l" in the name. If you're lucky enough to get a real mom in your sights, stop her and make her your friend. Shoot her with a Taser if you must, but don't let her escape without at least getting her e-mail address. Believe me, she is a rarer sight than Kirstie Allie eating a vegetable.

But how, you ask. How do I do it? How do I find a mom friend who's right for me, and once I do, how do I snare myself such a gem? Well, you must think of it as you would dating. You need to have an approach. First off, you can't seem too needy. Needy is a turnoff. Yes, I know we all felt that way when we first had a baby, but let's be real, the other moms can smell it on you like a fertilized lawn. They will sense it and think, *Ewww . . . I hope I never acted that desperate to belong.* And they did. But seeing it reminds them of that feeling. So you have to play it cool—but not too cool. You want to strike the right balance: interested but not eager. It's kind of tough, so I suggest you start getting practice while your baby is young—like pre-conception.

I met a woman at Target (new-mom headquarters)

when my baby was ten weeks old. I was with my mother shopping for diapers. My daughter seemed a little snug in her newborn-size Pampers, but I was torn between the size 2s or the size 1-2s. At more than one hundred diapers per box it seemed like a huge commitment. (I like commitment as much as a nineteen-year-old frat boy does.) What if I found out 1-2s were too small? But the 2s might be too big. So I fretted. I tried my old trick, What Would Gwyneth Do? But that didn't help. I mean, she named her baby Apple, so I couldn't trust her anymore.

Suddenly, out of the corner of my eye, I spotted a box of the exact diapers I was obsessing about. And when I looked up, I realized the diapers were sitting in the cart of a woman I needed to be friends with. She had long, straight hair (distinctly unmomlike); was dressed in baggy overalls with little paint splotches; and had on very artsy-looking glasses. I could tell from her very cool yet slightly hippie vibe that this was a woman who knew her way around a pot brownie. But slightly more important, her baby looked the same age as mine! I had to know this woman! But I was too shy and the thoughts started racing. Would she like me? Did she need a new friend? Did I look like crap? Of course I did. I was in my standard new-mom getup of maternity jeans with their telltale elastic waistband, and a three-dollar tank top, and my hair hadn't been washed since my last Lamaze class. I tried not to think about that.

Luckily, in this case I had a wingman—my mother, who flew right into pimp mode. She swaggered over to my future soul mate, got right up in her face, and, bad as you wanna be, asked, "So, how old is *your* baby?"

My future BFF replied, "Ten weeks."

"My granddaughter is the exact same age. Her mother is right here."

I pretended to be closing in on a very important decision regarding sugarless gum, and then I slowly walked over, trying my hardest to seem nonchalant, as though I already had a zillion new-mom friends. But when she confidently reached out her hand and said, "Hi, I'm Julie," I swooned.

We started talking. My mother and my new friend's husband faded into the background as we counted down the Top 40 new-mom classic topics, including diapers, lack of sleep, car seats, and height and weight (the babies', not ours). We talked and talked for what seemed like forever. Or until we both got through the line. Then we stood there with our purchases, not knowing what to do. I knew I had to see her again. But I didn't want to make the first move. Finally she said, "Maybe we should get together sometime." She handed me her card. "Call me."

Yes! I promised I would.

The second my mom and I were out of the store and into the parking garage, I pulled Julie's card out of my pocket and checked it out. Whoa, this woman worked at a high-profile magazine. She had a job! She was definitely a keeper. I waited the requisite new-mom week to call her, we made a plan, and, best of all, she didn't bring her mom.

New-Mom Pickup Lines

Beginner

How old is your baby?

Who's your pediatrician?

What kind of SUV do you drive?

What's your baby's sign?

Boy or girl?

More Advanced

Have you had sex yet? Want to? Me neither!

Wanna see my C-sec scar?

Excuse me, but is your baby a model?

You look like you've taken off your pregnancy weight and *then some*!

Are you single, or is your finger just still too swollen for your ring?

She sure is cute. Are you keeping her?

Do you still leak a little pee when you laugh?

Can I bum a Paxil?

Park Politics

You stroll your baby into the park for the first time, as nervous as you were on your first day of high school. You want to look your best. Old Navy maternity sweatpants? Check. Peg Perego umbrella stroller? Check. Baseball cap for unwashed hair? Check. Baby? Oh damn, hang on. Okay, check.

You glance around, hoping to make a connection, fearful of seeming too eager, too desperate.

The park: No other venue draws as many different moms together in one large mass of swings, slides, and status strollers. The park can be your haven, a place for your ankle-biter to get out from under you and socialize with their Pampers-wearing peers, while you tentatively seek out the company of other mothers, women who understand exactly what you're going through and can possibly offer up a bit of wisdom, a bit of support, and the occasional nugget of non-baby-related conversation. But your initial venture into the park can feel like a foray back into the palm-sweating insecure days of adolescence.

And if your postbaby social life is like high school, the park is like the high school cafeteria.

As you figure out where you'll fit in, you'll need to pick a bench next to the playground as carefully as you'd choose your lunch table.

Some moms can be really friendly and nice, offering up exciting info, such as "My baby's the same age as yours and she loves string cheese," before you've even been properly introduced. But if you feel like not everyone is welcoming you into the Breeders' World with open arms, you're not being paranoid. Some bitchy moms may try to make a new mom feel excluded from the club, as if there were more to joining than ditching your diaphragm.

Yup, certain moms can be a tough crowd. When you stagger into the park at nine a.m., tired and just looking for a friendly face, they'll see how tired you are and give you a rueful smile, as if to say, "I don't know why you're having trouble getting your baby to sleep. Maybe you're not getting the hang of this yet."

In moments like this remember that you will eventually find great friends . . . or at least one, but just as it was on your first day of navigating the cliques in high school, it's best to scope out the players before joining a team.

Although there will always be a handful of genuinely nice, normal moms simply trying to get through a day, keep a watchful eye out for these various subspecies of mommies found in a park on any given morning:

Alpha Mom—Alpha Mom probably gave up a major corporate job to be a full-time mom, and has plunged the aggression (and possible rage at having been born with ovaries) that had fueled her rise into upper middle management into a fierce obsession with child rearing. Realizing that knowledge is power, she's spent more time in the Barnes & Noble parenting section than anyone else. This mom considers herself the "baby whisperer," and given any opportunity, insists on dispensing her critiques on a wide range of your parenting decisions. She probably played softball in high school, and the competitive spirit still remains. Sure, her current sport may be only Bikram yoga, but she can sweat the shit out of any woman out there! So while you're still getting your parenting sea legs, it's best to keep a good distance between you and Alpha's forceful opinions, lest you get strong-armed into her ideas about everything from preschools to parenting philosophies.

Gossipy Mom—This mom starts every conversation with a stage-whispered "Soooo, you'll never guess what I heard!" She knows everyone at the park as well as everyone in the neighborhood and the surrounding three area codes. She has her own verbally distributed newsletter with features such as Who's Pregnant Again, Who's Legally Separated, and Who's Going Back to Work Part-Time. Although she can certainly be entertaining, this mom can get old real fast. But don't rule out a friendship with her—you need her for neighborhood information, and she needs you for . . . neighborhood information.

Drama Mama—"Oh my God, I need a root canal and my insurance ran out, like, just last week. Can you believe it? Plus, my car got broken into two years ago, but I'm having posttraumatic stress/anxiety attack flashbacks and a nightmare or two, so can you recommend a therapist I can speak to who will work with me on a sliding scale 'cause did I mention my insurance ran out?" If I were you, I would avoid this one like the latest season of *Big Brother*. Sure it can be a diversion to your most recent potty-training setback, but believe me, this one is a bottomless pit.

Bitchy Mom—Like Scientologists or new STDs, this mommy is more than irritating. She gives sneers out like Tic Tacs, and if you dare try to integrate yourself into a conversation she's having with another mom, she will look at you as if she's gotten a whiff of tuna salad that has just turned. Naturally submissive, she's a direct disciple of Alpha Mom, and has few opinions of her own. It's tough to do, but you need to stand up to her. Backing down from Bitchy Mom will only make her worse, while standing up to her will confuse her and eventually win her over. Take comfort in the fact that, just as in high school, this woman is mean because she's insecure. Plus, with her bad attitude, you can tell that she wouldn't know an orgasm if she sat on one.

Rich Mom—You probably won't ever speak to her directly, but you may get to know her children's Spanish-speaking caretaker, Consuela. Oh yeah, even though she doesn't work an hour a week, she still has full-time child care. If she does happen to swing by the park, you'll recognize her by her perfectly manicured acrylics, expensive diaper bag, and paid-for breasts. If you don't want to talk to her, stay in the sandbox. It's off-limits to her in her high heels. Someone else at the park may be having sex with her husband. . . . Gossipy Mom will be sure to fill you in.

Student Council Mom—This woman attends more community meetings than a newly sober alcoholic, refers to everyone as "gang," and is on a committee to have speed bumps put in the road on her street. If there's anything that needs organizing, she's the first one to volunteer (and sometimes the only one). She is also constantly late for her kid's next activity (thank God her four-year-old has a Palm Pilot), has perfect little snacks in perfect little containers, and weighs less than her six-year-old. At first glance you may mistake her for Alpha Mom, but unlike Alpha she actually would be your friend—if she didn't need to bake seventeen dozen cookies for the neighborhood bake sale next week! Gotta go!

Safety Patrol Mom—If this paranoid mommy could wear a bright orange utility belt filled with emergency items, she would. Try not to get pulled into any in-depth discussions with this mom—her obsession is contagious. It's difficult to have a conversation with her anyway, because she'll be way too busy chasing her two-year-old around as though he were made of bone china. If another child takes his toy, she's off the bench faster than Carl Lewis to snatch it back and give an impromptu lesson to the other child about sharing. She's equally worried about grass, falling leaves, and sex offenders. If there's a study that came out two minutes ago on the dangers of lead poisoning from willow trees, she'll have already read up on it, have had her child tested, and strongly suggest you do the same. Her catchphrase is "Not around the baby!" Expect to hear it when you accidentally refer to Alpha Mom as a cunt in Keds.

Crunchy Mom—She carries a hemp diaper bag, uses cloth diapers, makes all her own healthy baby food (for which she has endless recipes), and spends quality park time lecturing on recycling. Her earth-friendly deodorant kicks out at about seventy degrees, but she's so well meaning that even Gossipy Mom gives her a pass. Crunchy Mom loves a cause, so you'll rarely see her without a petition in her hand. On the plus side, she usually carries extra healthy snacks that she will offer to your kid. On the negative side, those snacks are usually made of tofu or bulgur wheat. If you're bored, Crunchy Mom is always up for a rousing debate on childhood vaccinations. If you want to make her your friend, offer to let her come over and feng shui your baby's room.

Burnout Mom—This mom has more than one kid, maybe four. Probably at one time a Safety Patrol Mom, now way overmedicated, she's become the most laid-back woman at the park. No matter what the weather this woman always shows up. A hurricane could sweep through, and she would continue on with her story undeterred. You will be way more worried about her kid's well-being than she is. In fact, if her kid falls off of the monkey bars and cracks his head open, she'll remain perfectly calm. Probably because she didn't notice it happen—she was midway through a story about the fight she got into with the contractors working on her house. When the piercing screaming finally gets her attention, she will brush her kid off with a "You're fine, you're fine."

Freshman Mom—Nonthreatening and friendly as a golden retriever puppy, this mom has just had what is undoubtedly her first baby, and she is open to bad influences, as you were. You can recognize her because her baby is way too young to take to the park, she has a wide-eyed expression, and she is willing to talk to anyone, including the guy who spears the leaves and puts them in the trash. Please keep in mind that you were this woman at some point probably not too long ago, and if your baby is twelve weeks old, you will be a wealth of information and helpful advice to someone with a baby who is only three weeks old. Even a few months can make a big difference in helping a new mom make her transition to full-fledged motherhood. Go to her. She needs you.

Once you get the lay of the land, you'll see that what you once worried was a clique you couldn't penetrate is actually a group of moms as unsure about everything as you are. In that way it really is more like high school than you ever thought. Confidence rules the park. And like in school, once you aren't trying too hard, those moms will be coming to you for answers.

In fact, be careful: If you show a glimmer of personality, you may become a mom-magnet for women like me who are starved for amusing conversation. Your openness and consistency will draw other moms in to the point that we will call you at all hours and instant-message you within an inch of your free time. Your playdate dance card will quickly fill up, and you may even need to drop out of sight for a while. Yes, you will become the queen bee of all the cliques, the one we all want and the one we all want to be: **Popular Mom**.

Good luck.

Married Mommy, Single Friends

Remember those people you used to talk to every day? The ones who still make an attempt to e-mail you once in a while? The ones who knew you even before you were married? The ones who *don't* have a baby? Not ringing a bell? Um, how about the ones who threw your damn baby shower? See, now it's slowly coming back to you. Yes, I'm talking about your single girlfriends.

It may seem absurd now, but you used to spend time with people who had no children. Since you had a baby, your old friendships are probably wasting away faster than your postnursing breasts. Look, I know you're tired. It's exhausting teaching your little one how to say "milk" in baby sign language, driving to the grocery store nineteen times a day, and deciding which take-out menu to order from, but no matter how hectic your life gets, you still need your friends.

I also get that new moms are as vital to your current lifestyle as spray-tan is to a stripper, but don't underestimate the value of the kidless. They can be a valuable resource. They know what's good on TV these days, which celebrities are in rehab, and whether or not you still need to lose more pregnancy weight (you do). But more important, your prebaby pals are a reminder that you used to have an identity before your baby came along. They know you once flashed truckers all the way from Seattle to Saint Louis and that your "Vegas name" is Blossom.

Not all your friendships with child-free buddies will make the transition. Some bonds were based on common interests that you no longer share, and those friendships may be gone for good. The friend you once spent hours comparing bad eHarmony dating stories with may start feeling a bit pathetic when she still calls you at midnight to bitch about the nebbishy guy she went out with, even though his picture made him look like an older, balder version of Jason Alexander. Likewise, the free spirit you shared a tent with when you followed the Grateful Dead for two years, who now attends Phish concerts religiously, may not seem quite as appealing to you—unless selling hash brownies out of a '73 Dodge conversion van is an activity you'd like to share with your kids.

I doubt you've managed to stay friends with those people for *this* long, but if you're still hanging on, it's time to make a clean break. It's better this way.

But then there are other kidless friends, friends who have stuck with you through good times and bad times, the ones who didn't mind being seen with you when you went through your "white cowboy boots" phase for three years, and friends who stuck around when you moved in with that guy who was *clearly* an alcoholic and who was eventually arrested for shoplifting. (Of course you still didn't break up with him. That would require self-esteem. No, first he cheated on you, *then* you broke up with him—and got back together with him and broke up with him one more time.)

These are the kinds of true friends who want to share your maternal experience, but not have it redefine your whole relationship. They've proven they can withstand change, but now that you have a child, these friends require a little more nurturing.

Be respectful of these friends right from the start of your journey into motherhood. One easy way you can do that is to *not* refer to it as a "journey." That will go a long way in helping you maintain your friendship.

Most important, realize that when you're pregnant, your single buds may not be as interested in the whole process as you are. Primarily they'll be fascinated with how fat you're getting, and that's it. The idea of an actual person growing inside you will be much too disconcerting an image for someone who knows you best as "the girl who'd kill to bone Brad Pitt." In keeping with the spirit of their disinterest, your mass e-mails of the ultrasound pictures of your fetus probably won't be appreciated. It's best to save those for immediate family members and that one ex-boyfriend who's having trouble getting the message that it's truly over.

Next, you know how your new-mom companions are never available to go out? Well, news flash, you aren't much either. If you have any single girlfriends left, and they are willing to stay friends with you despite your new all-consuming responsibility, you need to make an effort and meet them halfway! For the friends who are worth it you've gotta get your ass in the game once in a while. No one expects you to go out every night or even every week, and they know you're not available on the spur of the moment. But now and then, *even if you don't feel like it*, you must force yourself to go out and have fun without your baby, or you'll shortly be dropped from everyone's Evite lists. I know it's unfair, I know they "just don't understand," but the reality is, they don't. Even if you have to cram your crazy party night into an hour and forty-five minutes, including drive time, and physically restrain yourself from talking only about your baby and your crappy sex life, it's worth it—if only to be around people who love you for more than your lactation abilities.

Remember your kidless friends have lives of their own, even if their interests suddenly seem shallow to you while you're in the throes of new motherhood. Your friend who just went on a fourth date with a guy who couldn't be less appropriate isn't looking for a sermon right now. She doesn't want to hear "I'm sorry, but that guy isn't good dad material." Try to focus on what your old friends are doing without filtering everything through your "parent prism." Your friends need to feel assured that you're still you, just with shapeless boobs.

After you have a kid, as overwhelmed as you are, ironically you may need to meet your childless friends more than halfway, because they haven't gone through a change, *you have*.

Okay, so you can't drop all and fly to Vegas for your best friend's bachelorette blowout, but you can still buy her the biggest turbocharged dildo the world has ever seen! Yeah, I said that, and I'm a mom!

Between Gymboree, Mommy & Me, and every other baby-oriented activity you're signed up for, you will be spending plenty of time with other moms who are dealing with the same issues you are. Occasionally you will need a break from talking about what your baby should be eating, how often he's pooping, and whether or not you're residing in a decent school district. The kidless are perfect for this because they don't give a rat's ass about anyone under three feet tall. While it's difficult for a lot of your new mommy friends to get off the topic of babies, your kidless companions will have more trouble staying on it.

Over drinks your polite kidless friend will undoubtedly ask, "How's the baby?" And you'll reply with all the fake modesty you can muster, "Oh, she's fine. Thanks for asking. But enough about me and my creating a whole new life, how are *you?*" To which Polite Kidless will say, "Ugh, I got stood up last night!" and you'll cut in, "Oh my God, speaking of stood up, my baby pulled up to a stand for the very first time the other night. It's so crazy! I was starting to think she was behind developmentally, but here's what happened . . . we're sitting in the tub, together like always, playing with her yellow rubber ducky—she loves to play with her rubber ducky. A lot of times I'll sing the rubber ducky song to her, and I swear it seems like she's trying to sing it right along with me. I really need to get more bath toys for her, because we only have a few. Anyhoo . . . suddenly she grabs on to the side of the tub and she's UP—just like that. I couldn't believe it!"

At this point your friend will be working on her third Mojito and may throw in a requisite "Wow. That's fantastic. I need to come by and see her sometime. Truly." You may mistake this for genuine interest, but in actuality your friend is long gone to her happy place.

She might make an attempt to steer the conversation to her latest boozy one-night stand or to the coup she pulled off at her high-powered job that you can't quite recall anymore. Or she'll tell you that she went rock climbing, and how beautiful it was to commune with nature. Although I doubt you have any friends who would really spend happy hour talking about nature, unless, of course, they're lesbians.

Realize that when they're talking about their own lives, it is not the time to try to convince them how empty their life is without a child, and recruit them onto the baby bandwagon like an Amway rep. This will only succeed in making them leave you with the check.

Not everyone wants children or is even interested in them. You must try to respect this and be reasonable with your expectations. That doesn't mean you have to swallow all comments about how much you love your baby. But it does mean putting on the brakes before asking your kidless friends to help you design handmade cowboy-themed invitations to your son's first birthday party that say "We'll Have a Rootin' Tootin' Good Time!" Trust me, that will sound about as fun to them as alphabetizing your DVD collection. Besides, tedious crap like this is why you have a husband.

Once you've learned to show your unencumbered companions that you can indeed still relate to their single lives, you'll likely expect them to instantly reciprocate by understanding and adapting to your new schedule. This may be tough at first because they won't understand that you simply must be home when there's a teething situation or that it's impossible to leave the house until you've bribed your two-year-old to finish his lunch.

I was once four hours late to a barbecue because of my daughter's refusal to take a nap. Knowing it would be a disaster to bring her out in public without her morning snooze, I was held hostage at home most of the day. By the time I made it to my friend's house, most of the tacos were eaten (it was a So Cal BBQ). At first my friend was disappointed. But after I pointed out how much less time my daughter would have to accidentally mush black beans into her carpet, she perked right up.

No matter what you do, some of your kidless gang won't want to be friends anymore. This can happen for myriad reasons: They may find your one-track baby mind annoying and feel that you're no longer as enjoyable to hang out with; they may feel left out and worry that you don't care about them; or they may even simply be jealous that you have what they want, and they may lash out in the only way they know how: by blowing you off.

Just know that once they have a baby of their own, they will feel like a complete ass. I should know. I was that person. During my single years I deleted a couple of friends as if they were e-mail advertisements for organic Viagra. I felt they didn't "get" me anymore or have enough time for me once they had a baby. Extremely selfish, I know. But in my defense I was only in my early thirties. What does anyone know about life at that age?

The wonderful thing about mothers is that they are champions at forgiveness. It comes with the territory. Those very same women I took off my speed-dial as soon as they popped out a kid were right there for me when they found out that I was having a baby. No questions asked. Did I deserve it? Probably not, but those women are some of my closest friends, now that we're all parents. And following their example, when my friends who blew me off eventually announce their own pregnancies, I will be there by their side, paying it forward. Except for the times I'm out partying with kidless homies like it's 1999.

Good-bye, Hot Wifey;
Hello, Mommy

I can't stand those people who love to issue ridiculous warnings before you have kids. You know the ones: They feel the need to let you know how tough having kids is on a marriage—with the whole "loss of freedom," "no alone time with your husband," and "say good-bye to your sex drive." Blah, blah, blah. Hey, how about fewer downers and a few more "You're about the hottest seven-months-pregnant woman I've ever seen!"

I'm loath to admit it, but the dire forecast turns out to be true. Yes, I was sure it wouldn't happen to me, but even if you're Catherine Zeta Jones, there's no getting around it. Having a baby changes your body, mind, and marriage.

While I was pregnant, I was positive we would side-step this pitfall when planning life as a threesome. After all, my husband and I were different from other couples we knew who had kids. We genuinely enjoyed each other's company, had a lot in common, and seldom fought in public. The loss of freedom thing didn't scare us at all because we didn't need to be able to do things at the spur of the moment to have fun. In fact, one of the main things we have in common is, we're *not* spontaneous! We spit in the face of spontaneity! We welcomed an excuse to stay home. Our favorite activity was hanging out every night watching bad reality television. How different would it be with a baby? We'd just have to scooch over and make some extra room on the couch.

Once I had the baby, that fantasy lasted about as long as the talented fat chicks on *American Idol*.

It will happen to you too. The moment you come home from the hospital, you'll notice that things have changed even more than anticipated. You're suddenly a mom and you must adjust to your new mother role. What you are about to experience is a normal right of passage, but it can be hell on your love life. Picture your marriage as a quiet country lane and your baby as a Hummer. No matter how careful you are, there's gonna be roadkill.

A new baby is all-consuming both mentally and physically. Your mate may find you are more interested in your baby than in him: less fun, more bitchy, and just "not like yourself." And you *aren't* yourself. When you look in the mirror, you won't recognize the person looking back at you. When the *fuck* did you become a size *fourteen*? Sorry, but lack of sleep makes you edgy. You will be feeling like a simmering pot of hormonal, distant, frustrated, resentful, and unsexy stew. Mmm. Tasty.

Primarily I found myself wondering, *How the hell am I supposed to be fun when there's always something in my in-box?*

(Keep in mind that it was *at least* six months after the delivery before "in-box" could again be safely used around my house as a sophomoric sexual metaphor.) When it came to baby care, no matter how egalitarian my marriage was, I had the overwhelming feeling that I, and I alone, was in charge of this tiny and fragile new life. Regardless of how many baby-care hours my husband logged, I still felt like I was doing it all alone. And I expressed that. Over and over. And my husband thought I was being a martyr. This is completely normal. It's in our maternal blood. I don't care how laid back you were before having a baby. As a brand-new mother, for the first few weeks you'll be at Def Con 2, on high alert, aware of your baby's slightest twitch or cough. Assume Def Con 1 if you're breast-feeding. Believe me, it will take about six glasses of pinot grigio to get you back down to Def Con 3, a pervasive feeling of moderate unfocused agitation. Learn to enjoy it, because for the next decade that's your new definition of "relaxed."

I knew every second of every day where my baby was, and what she was doing, as if I'd been equipped with a mental LoJack that was always monitoring her. I know my husband was devoted to our new baby with every fiber of his being, but I couldn't believe his ability to walk in and out of a room with ease. I'd watch in fascination as he'd go from the living room to the kitchen to the bathroom and into the bedroom to watch TV, as though he *didn't even have a baby*! I was annoyed at his ability to relax. I felt like saying, "Didn't you get the memo? WE'RE PARENTS NOW! LOOK ALIVE!"

In actuality my husband worked his ass off to help. But I still had no problem feeling resentful, because when he did something with the baby it felt like he was doing me a favor. He'd innocently ask me a question like, "Do you want me to give the baby her bottle?" or "Should I take her for a little while?" and I would be thinking, *She's your baby too! Don't ask, just do it.*

Your husband will probably look to you for the answers to all questions baby, and you won't have a clue either, so you'll make them up, thus sealing your fate as the go-to baby expert. And now you really will feel like it's all up to you. It's a vicious cycle. At some point you might lose it and cry, "Who do I have to blow to get some housework help around here?" Your husband will immediately answer "Me," and you'll say, "Oh, never mind."

Need I say that all this stress and anxiety isn't exactly an aphrodisiac? During this time I think most women consider sex the next-to-last thing they feel like doing—the very last being laundry. Luckily, for the first six weeks or so, you aren't allowed to have sex, so you won't have to worry. And for the next couple of weeks after that you will *pretend* you still can't have sex . . . doctor's orders. But as the dry spell continues month after month, your husband may start to get a little concerned that maybe your vagina fell off.

It's tough to get in the mood. Even when your husband takes the baby for the whole day, it does not count as foreplay. Although the books say it will, it won't get you in the mood for sex, which was probably his goal in the first place. You might say to him, "You know what would be really relaxing? What I fantasize about? *A nap.* Let's start there and work our way up to a blow job in a few more months."

Lots of magazines offer wonderful things to do to get yourself in the mood for sex after a baby: taking a bath in rose petals, lighting scented candles, or slow dancing together. Those suggestions are great if you're thirteen or have a lifetime subscription to *Martha Stewart Living*, but remember that Martha isn't volunteering to drop by and calm your sleepless seven-week-old while you screw.

Bottom line, you may not feel at all open to the idea of having sex for quite a while. So you should respect the way you feel, and refuse to have sex until you're truly in the mood again, right? Wrong! This will veer you right off the healthy relationship path.

A lot of women think if they don't feel like having sex, they shouldn't force themselves. But think about it; when you stop going to the gym for a couple of months, about the last thing you want to do is spend forty-five minutes on the treadmill, right? But you take a good hard look at your flabby thighs and you make yourself go and do it. Well, think of your sex life as flabby. It's not going to tone itself! Just as with the gym, you may have to force yourself the first time back.

One thing that helps is to set a time to do it and stick with it. You can also mentally psych yourself up . . . with wine. Once you start, you will slowly get into it, and by the time you're done, just as with the gym, you'll be thinking, *Why don't I do this more often?* The only difference between sex and the gym is, it isn't frowned upon to have a few glasses of wine before sex. Take my word for it, I've been eighty-sixed from quite a few sports clubs.

Another thing that will help you and your husband stay sexually motivated is if you make a concerted effort not to fall prey to the Mommy Look. Some moms have been preprogrammed to believe that motherhood requires a swift transformation to a vaguely asexual look, dress, and posture. For the record, because you are a mom does not mean it's mandatory to have a nondescript haircut that hits "slightly below the ears" and to wear relaxed-fitting jeans that hit "slightly above the waist."

What is it about becoming a mom that makes certain things that were never a good idea before suddenly seem appealing—like bangs or green eye shadow? You can't blame this on baby weight, because long after the last pounds have been shed, the sensible hair, the flats, and the minivan jeans remain firmly in place.

I sadly recall Kyra, the punk bartender who used to give me free tequila shots. Well, once sperm met egg, good-bye Bettie Page do and ripped *The Cramps* T-shirt, hello sensible hair helmet and sweater set. This kind of behavior does not help your husband see you as a sexual being, and definitely doesn't help you get in the mood to be seen as a sexual being. And right now you can use all the help you can get.

So go ahead and leave your hair long. Or if it's already short, go shorter and spikier. You don't have to be Pam Anderson, but try to at least stay you and keep it in this decade.

A lot of men are trying their hapless best, in their way, to make you happy. You have to make a concerted effort to not mark your husband as the enemy, especially if he's trying to help. It's quite natural to feel that your husband doesn't know how to do things for the baby as well as you do. He may not. But if you tell your husband he's doing it wrong, he won't do it anymore. And doing it wrong is still preferable to not doing it at all.

Quiz Yourself

You've asked your husband to please get the baby dressed. A half hour later he presents your baby to you wearing a purple flowered dress, yellow polka-dot socks, and a red baseball cap. Do you say:

A) "Are you mixing your meds again?"
   or
B) "Wow, what a creative color combo! And such a great look for our son. Thank you, honey."

The correct answer is *A*, but the one you should give your husband is *B*. This will award your husband confidence, build his self-esteem, and make him feel a teeny bit gay.

Try giving your husband one specific job to do with the baby. I turned over the "putting the shorty to bed" duties. This included giving her a bottle and getting her to sleep. At first he seemed uncomfortable, but in no time flat he became the resident sleep expert. I'd try to put her to bed once in a while, and he'd pop in to tell me I wasn't doing it right. She doesn't like to hold the bottle "quite like that," she needs *this* stuffed animal not *that* one. Suddenly he's an infantologist. All this time I though he was a writer, but no—infantologist.

Here's the good news. The first few months with a baby are like a high-wire act. All focus must be on the baby. But once those months have passed, the strain will lift and having a baby can actually bring you closer as a family. You two are responsible for a little being. Together! A team! And that is a strong, unbreakable bond. Look how many times Eminem has gotten back together with Kim Mathers. He writes songs about wanting to kill her, but then they work it out. Why? They have a child together. And isn't that what it's all about? Powerful stuff.

Questions Not to Ask Your Husband in the First Year After You've Had a Baby, Unless You're Prepared to Hear the Answer

"Am I stripper material?"

"Do you think our babysitter is cute?"

"Should I get liposuction?"

"Which diaper bag do you like better?"

"If you weren't weighed down by a wife and kid, who would you have sex with?"

"Are you masturbating—*again?*"

"Can you remember when I last showered?"

"Should I get a job?"

"Be honest, who is hotter: me or Mandy Moore?"

"Okay, make good. Who's hotter: me or Lesley Stahl?"

"Does it bother you that I haven't waxed in eighteen months?"

Fun Things to Keep the Magic Alive

Have a contest to see who can go the longest without brushing their teeth.

Accuse him of having an affair, and then say, "Just kidding!" Men love that.

Go all out one night and really take the time to set a beautiful table for your take-out meal.

See if you can sit through *Jackass: The Movie* one more time.

Drop a quarter in a jar every time you fight over who last woke up with the baby.

Secretly agree that all couples who choose not to have children *obviously* don't have as strong a marriage as you have. Feel sorry for them.

Talk often about going camping someday.

Sleep on the couch for a month to see if he misses you.

Make a CD of songs the two of you both love, and then play it VERY SOFTLY BECAUSE CAN'T YOU TELL THE BABY'S SLEEPING??

Taking Off the Baby Weight

Just for the record I have some badass jeans in my closet. Jeans I haven't been able to wear in, well, I'm embarrassed to say how long. I gained fifty-five pounds when I was pregnant. But before I got knocked up, I was at my lowest weight ever, and feeling pretty darn pleased with myself. Of course, even at my slimmest I had what a black man might call a slammin' boo-tay and what a white man might call cellulite.

Barring pregnancy, my weight has fluctuated at least twenty pounds. The lowest was when working out and eating healthily, and the highest was during a particularly bad year working as a clerk at an insurance company (insane boredom, vending machines, and a boss with a Napoleon complex all played important roles). Once I dropped the job, I quickly dropped the pounds. But the point is, I've never had a weight problem per se. I've always paid attention to the fat and calorie contents of the foods I eat, but tried not to be crazy about it. Sure, I'd have the Cobb salad but "dressing on the side please."

But when I was pregnant, I was hungry. Not, "Hey, wanna split a muffin?" hungry. More like, "Get your own muffin, bitch" hungry. So, spitting in the face of Los Angeles' obsession with thin, I ate everything I wanted. Even with no personal trainer waiting in the wings to help me shed the weight, as a lot of famous people have, I didn't stop to worry. I wolfed down pasta like I was training for a marathon. I even ate things I didn't know I wanted. For instance, I had a craving for hot wings that was so strong it nearly required medical attention. I honestly didn't know where to get them. I had to track down a recipe online and make my own. In the past when it came to hot wings, I was the way a lot of people are with pot—"Hey, I'd have some if it were around, but I'd never actually *buy* it on my own." But this was different: It wasn't just about me, and I had to be the bigger person. I mean, obviously my baby was craving chicken wings, and who was I to deny her? So, for the sake of my growing fetus, I ate chicken wings—about a kilo of chicken wings.

Looking back, I can see I was in denial. Having never been pregnant before, I figured that once the baby came out, the weight would come right off, and I would pretty quickly be thin again. I convinced myself that most of the weight was baby, placenta (I hear those things can weigh more than a Thanksgiving turkey), and really heavy clothes, and anything else was *obviously* water weight.

After the baby came out, three weeks went by before my first doctor's appointment. I got weighed—and had lost twenty-five pounds! Yeah! Like I said, mostly water weight. I don't know why women are so freaked out about this issue.

And then nothing. I didn't lose another pound for a long, long time. Even though I switched from Miller Genuine Draft to Miller Lite! How hard can it be to lose a little water weight? The answer to that question is: pretty frickin' hard.

At first when the scale wasn't moving south, I didn't worry much, because I had other things on my mind, like my BABY. Plus, my feeling is, unless your movie's shooting next week, you've got some time. So, still in maternity jeans when my baby was a couple of months old, I decided to kick it up a notch and start back to the gym, taking things *slowly*.

A few months later I'd lost only a couple more pounds. Despite the fact that my prepregnancy workout included at least an hour on the Precor machines, and now my gym routine consisted of a PowerBar and thirty minutes in the sauna, I was stumped. I started to wonder what was up. Had pregnancy thrown my metabolism completely out of whack for good? Or maybe I had a thyroid problem! That had to be it. I made a mental note to ask my doctor about it.

The way I was latching on to excuses, you'd think that I'd eaten all those chicken wings and french fries in a blackout.

After finding out there was nothing wrong with my thyroid—or so the repeated tests would have had me believe—I decided that I would have to do something about the twenty-five extra pounds that weren't melting away as expected. I mean, not diet. I wasn't desperate . . . yet.

The common advice wasn't helping. You've heard it: "Focus on the baby and the weight will come off." Really? Focus on the baby? Unless the baby is an aerobics instructor, I'm not sure how that's supposed to work. And it doesn't work to substitute something else, like . . . focus on the television screen and the weight will come off.

But still I figured there must be some kind of shortcut—a diet especially for women like me. That is, women with my *special* condition. Women who'd just had a baby, oh, at this point, eight months ago.

I didn't have to look far. There is no shortage of books and DVDs profiting from this very issue. One called *From Baby to Bikini* was written by two *men!* How perfect. I guess, like so many other things, men are naturally better at taking off baby weight. After writing this book I plan to write one to help men, called *From Beer Gut to Speedo*. Send it to a man you love.

There's another popular book out there with a truly uplifting message: "If you don't lose all your pregnancy weight in the first six months, you never will." Great. If that doesn't have you reaching for the Chips Ahoy!, I guess you'd better start doing those power squats while they're cutting the umbilical cord. When you pack your overnight bag for the hospital, don't forget the arm and ankle weights!

You don't need a book to take off the baby weight. I found out the hard way that losing weight after you have a baby is *exactly* like losing weight at other times. You have to eat less and exercise more. I know, radical notion. There's no easy fix. Walking once a week ain't gonna cut it. You've gotta kick it old school and go to the gym and sweat.

I know it's harder to find the time or motivation to work out when you first have a baby. Some of you may prefer to bitch about your ass and grab a handful of your back fat to show your husband, while saying "Look! Look how huge I am." By the way, shining a fluorescent light on your saddlebags doesn't work as foreplay. But once things calm down, like when your baby goes off to college, if it's important to you that you lose weight, you'll lose it.

Once you do decide to get serious about taking the weight off and working out, there are a couple of things you shouldn't pay attention to. The first one is celebrities. We've all heard about how celebrities gain a ton of weight but have a personal trainer on hand twenty-four hours a day, seven days a week, to lose it. Plus, they have nannies to take care of the babies while they stick to their workout regimes. But what you might not know is, the reason some of them look like they took the weight off overnight is . . . they did. Yeah, they weren't actually pregnant. Some celebs just pretend to get pregnant as a publicity stunt. Julia Roberts's twins? CGI.

Another thing to keep in mind is the whole "size fallacy" thing. Every time you see a woman on a talk show who has lost a lot of weight, they report being a ridiculously small size. If they went from 230 pounds down to 168, they are a "size 8." If they went from 180 down to 140, they are a "size 2." These women may feel fantastic about themselves, but they are not this size, at least not in a pair of jeans. And you don't have to be either.

Above all, you need to avoid those so-called friends who, without doing a thing, are back in their pre-pregnancy jeans, oh, about an hour after popping out their kid. I'm sure there are a few of them out there. Here's hoping they have horrible stretch marks—just to even things out.

One more thing. While you're still chunky, don't start buying yourself a bunch of new clothes. If you do, you may start feeling too comfortable at your new weight. Look, at some point either you will get motivated to work out and eat less or you'll be stuck wearing your JUST HAD A BABY! T-shirt for the first three years of your kid's life. And, by the way, once your baby is studying for the SATs, it's no longer baby weight. You're fat.

Mommy and Me, Me, Me

There came a time when my baby was about six months old that I realized that a trip to the grocery store didn't constitute a full day of activity in the outside world for either of us, even if one of us was sneaking samples from the bulk section. The brief walk around the block later in the day wasn't adding much either. (I'd try to make it around the whole neighborhood, but my cell phone kept running out of juice.) So, while sitting in my living room for the tenth straight day, I realized the time had come to consider some alternate entertainment options.

Up until this point I'd avoided organized baby activities. I've never been much of a joiner, and in the beginning I had a ready-made excuse—I could barely get the baby in and out of the car in less than an hour. Plus, I'd always been a bit closed-minded about these types of things. I'd hear people talking about Mommy & Me, and judging by the name alone it sounded like something I'd have absolutely no interest in. I couldn't help but think, *Your baby doesn't need to be making friends at three months old—you do! But not with people you'll meet at Mommy & Me.*

I imagined the worst: magenta-colored walls with enormous yellow suns painted on them, and mommies as perky as preschool teachers, nuzzling their little cuties in their laps, singing cherished children's songs that I wouldn't be able to recall even if there were a gun to my head. Especially if there were a gun to my head! A lot of women taking their mothering *very* seriously.

So I looked into some alternatives, and as it turns out, there's no shortage of organized activities for you and your cherub—provided you have unlimited time and money. You can sign your infant up for tiny baby gymnastics, Itsy Bitsy Yoga, dance classes, music classes, and, if you live in New York, you can sign your six-month-old up for Broadway Babies, so they can learn to drool their way through *Rent*. If you decide that a trip down your birth canal isn't enough of a workout for your newborn, there's even a swimming class that offers lessons for *one-day-old babies*. What the hell? That just seems like a waste of money. You know how newborns are, by the time the kid is thirty-six hours old, he'll have forgotten everything he learned.

After I reviewed my various options, Mommy & Me started to sound more and more tolerable, so I reluctantly signed up for a class at a local temple, put on my fanciest drawstring pants, and hoped for the best. Maybe I'd make a friend.

It turned out my initial fears were not unfounded.

The group consisted of about twelve women and their babies arranged in a big circle on large colorful mats on the floor. Each mat had a face depicting a different mood and the name of that mood, such as HAPPY, SAD, SHY.

I scanned the room for my best discreet exit strategy, and then planted myself and my baby on a GRUMPY mat nearby.

The woman who sat down on my right had a baby approximately the same age as mine, so we struck up a conversation, which immediately proved difficult because of an unfortunate neon sweatband around her forehead. After a few minutes of not knowing where to look, I turned to the woman on my left. It was then that I made a truly frightening discovery—she too had a neon sweatband! Imagine the Vegas odds on two out of twelve women in the same room having on the exact same fashion atrocity.

Luckily, right about the time I'd run out of places to focus, our "leader," a woman whose pleasant personality made up for a lack of expertise of any kind, asked who among us had "baby issues" they wanted to discuss. She hit pay dirt with this crowd. It seemed plenty of moms were champing at the bit to hear the advice a group of equally inexperienced women could give them regarding certain pressing concerns. My attitude was getting poorer by the minute.

We spent the next forty-five minutes exchanging information on scintillating topics such as Is Diaper Rash Really a Rash?, The Pros and Cons of Spending Extra Money on Dreft Detergent, and Are Pampers Really Better for Girls? If there hadn't been a leader present, perhaps we could have discussed more important mommy issues such as How to Clean Your Bathroom Without Actually Cleaning Your Bathroom, or Finding Time to Masturbate, but this was definitely all about the babies.

One woman giddily suggested that it might be a fun mommy activity for all of us to drive about forty miles out of town later that week to watch her get her new child car seat installed, and unbelievably, a few women actually seemed genuinely interested. I momentarily considered inviting everyone along for my next Pap smear but was scared I'd get some takers.

During this time my mind started to wander a bit. I glanced around to see if there were any moms who felt as out of their element as I did. I noticed one woman was wearing a pink tank top with the words "Brody's Mommy" spelled out in sequins, like she was some sort of Brody groupie. I wondered what this was all about. I love my baby too, but I've never felt the need to shout it from my breasts. Hey, I own my home, but I don't have that information bedazzled on the seat of my pants. Plus, I've never seen anyone wearing an I HAVE HERPES T-shirt. Yet I happen to know that one out of every six people carries the virus. Wouldn't that be much more helpful personal advertising?

It also occurred to me that I could get a group of mothers with babies around my baby's age together at one of our houses or a park—for free. This is officially called a playgroup. For a lot of women this is ideal, but I had to be realistic. I can't figure out how to fit a vegetable in with a pasta dish. There was no way I would be organizing a group of women and their babies to be in the same place at the same time—with snacks—on a weekly basis.

I snapped back to attention as we shifted to the entertainment portion of the class. Our leader opened her set with a couple of baby crowd-pleaser songs: "Open, Shut Them" and "Wheels on the Bus." It was as I'd feared, I didn't know any of the words to these songs and felt self-conscious and out of place. But as I scanned the room to see if anyone would notice if I snuck out, I finally caught the eye of a woman who looked as ill at ease as I did. She smiled at me and rolled her eyes. There, I'd made a friend. My work here was done. I figured I'd try to get my new buddy to ditch this group and go to the mall.

But when I looked down at the little wriggly baby in my lap, I saw that she was loving it: the atmosphere, the songs, the other babies. My little sweetie's eyes were lit up like Paris Hilton's in a Fendi shop. My heart melted, and I knew I was in for the long haul. She giggled her way through every baby song, clapping game, and nursery rhyme. I leaned in close, nuzzling her ear, and whispered, "You do know this means you will not be putting me in a home when I get old, right?"

Just when it seemed it couldn't get any cheesier, a couple of bird hand-puppets made an appearance. I think they were supposed to be birds, because of the "Two Little Blackbirds" song that accompanied them, but it was difficult to make a visual ID. These puppets looked like they'd been sewn by someone in the midst of a seizure, on a train . . . during an earthquake. Yet the babies responded like a bunch of sex starved blue-hairs at a Tom Jones concert. I could swear a couple of the babies were so excited they threw their Pampers into the middle of the room. It was downright embarrassing.

And then I realized something even more troubling. I was kind of into it in spite of myself, smiling and laughing along with my baby. I couldn't pinpoint the exact moment I'd gone over to the dark side, but it had happened.

Later in the parking lot it really sunk in as I strapped my exhausted baby into her car seat and yelled "See you next week" to Brody's mom as she drove away in a huge white Lexus with a vanity plate surrounded by flashing lights that read, naturally, BRODYSMOM. I knew with certainty that this wouldn't be the last time I'd be sacrificing my dignity in the name of motherhood. Yes, I'd be back at Mommy & Me next week. And the week after that.

But I wouldn't rule out a little private weekly play-group with my one new Mommy & Me friend at the nearby El Torito—free except for the price of four margaritas.

Out and About with Your Baby

When I see women out on the town with their babies, looking as nimble as Batman and Robin on a crime-fighting mission, I have to say that I feel jealous. There's a way these women have of hopping out of their Lincoln Navigator, swinging around to open the trunk, unfurling their stroller while collecting the baby as if the whole thing were choreographed by Bob Fosse.

One of the most daunting moments in the first few months was my inaugural social outing with my baby—a lunch with a couple other new moms.

For that excursion I started packing about a day and a half before, and if you'd seen the bags, you would've thought I was packing to join the Peace Corps. When I had finally gotten us loaded into the car and had started driving, I noticed that my hands were clammy on the steering wheel. I kept the radio turned down low for the first time since I'd learned to drive, and every single step with my brand-new, straight-out-of-the-packaging baby was overwhelming. I was in a state of constant anxiety.

Of course I hadn't bothered to practice opening and closing the stroller one handed, the way the baby book had suggested I should. My thinking was that the short time between my baby shower and my baby's arrival was way too precious to be wasted on practicing stroller technique. I had much more important issues to attend to, like programming the TiVo for while I was in the maternity ward, and visually scouting my body for new varicose veins. Plus I assumed I was way ahead of the game because I'd managed to get my husband to actually put the damn stroller together *before* I gave birth.

Well, that lunch outing turned out to be the longest two hours I ever spent traveling two miles. And to add insult to injury, I stayed for only about forty-five minutes before the baby got hungry, and I had to turn around and repeat the process to go home.

Even after you've mastered getting a newborn out of the house in less than four hours, it's still an ordeal to make your way through a normal set of errands with a fourteen-pound mood swing on your arm. A case in point: A few months later, on one of my thrice weekly trips to Target, I masterfully maneuvered the baby from the house, into the car seat, to the store, out of the car seat, into the stroller, and partway through the store. Then she started screaming. By this time, having had a little more practice, I realized that she was screaming because she now hated being in the stroller. No apparent reason for this sudden dislike, just not into it—and more than willing to let the entire store in on that fact. So to keep the peace and to end the knowing clucks I was hearing down every aisle, I needed to return to the car to get the BABYBJÖRN. But in order to strap on the Björn and fold up the stroller I needed to put the baby back in the car seat, where her screaming reached a pitch rarely heard other than on The Discovery Health Channel. She screamed until I was certain that concerned Target shoppers in the parking lot were dialing child protective services. Luckily, the phone line was probably busy with all the other moms in the same parking lot being reported for the same thing.

Finally I got the baby into her sling and quieted down, and I returned to the store, only to find my half-filled cart gone because forty minutes had passed and some Target employee had thoughtfully returned all my stuff to the shelves. Now that's service.

After this I considered myself a hardened vet, but I knew the incident wouldn't make future outings easier, merely less surprising.

The insane part of all this is that if you stay at home with your kid, after a while you will actually find yourself conjuring up errands to do with them, because even with all the prep work, running errands is more exciting than staying home. But, really, it's sort of a bonus for both of you. Around the time you're starting to feel like you're trapped in a diaper-scented prison, you'll find your baby is of the same mind, chafing under the constant watch of a warden who won't allow even fifteen minutes a day of unlimited pots and pans access.

But at this point, contrary to popular belief, you don't need to pack as much. I know a lot of women still stuff steamer trunks like they're going on the *Gilligan's Island* "three hour cruise," secretly thinking they might be stuck somewhere with their baby for eight seasons plus syndication. But the beauty of babies once they reach a year is, you can start packing light. You need a bottle if you're not breast-feeding, one outfit change, a diaper, a toy, and a few Cheerios in case there's trouble. Anything more than that is dead weight in my opinion.

When you take your baby out to a store, besides getting out of the house, your baby has a golden opportunity to flirt. Babies live for a chance to be around people who aren't you. They see you a lot, and what baby wouldn't love all the "What an adorable baby" comments they get from random strangers? In the right outfit babies can pull a lot of compliments, and only 2 percent of them are from sexual predators. Bonus!

Yes, soon your babies will take to going out on a daily basis and will quickly become full-on attention hos. Going out with them will be like hanging out at a bar with your one girlfriend who gets hammered and finds everyone attractive. She flirts indiscriminately, making each person think they have an equal chance of going home with her. It's up to you to keep an eye on those little suckers. One minute they're grinning at the store clerk and the next minute they're blowing kisses to a demented homeless guy. But hey, drunk chick or baby, either way, they're both getting carried out at the end of the night.

By the way, if you do choose to use one of those kid leashes, be careful. If your kid adapts to a leash at three, don't be surprised if they develop a disturbing fondness for it at thirty-three.

Once your kid gets a little older, going out does become easier, but don't let yourself get lulled into a false sense of security. A lot of mothers get cocky and start packing so light that they're just taunting the gods. One friend of mine went out with her eighteen-month-old after he'd had a big lunch, and she took nothing but her wallet. On the way back in the car she heard a funny noise and turned around to find her kid projectile vomiting. Not having a single change of clothes, she had to finish her trip with the kid totally nude and smelling like he'd spent a night in a frat house. Luckily, it brought back fond memories of her first dates with her husband.

So, yes, traveling with a baby is challenging even if it's only out to the mailbox. And maybe you can't take your baby to exotic locations, and Mommy & Me BOTOX has to wait a few years, but as you get the hang of getting out and about with your baby, I hear it can actually be enjoyable. Your choreography will eventually go from looking like a drunk ballerina to looking like *Swan Lake*. I, myself, am still at drunk ballerina. But hope springs eternal!

Planes, Trains, and Automobiles

After I became a mother, maybe the hardest adjustment I had to make was dealing with the fact that I'd changed sides in one of the most emotional battles dividing the nation today. I'd joined one of the most despised special interest groups ever to feel the wrath of angry stares and implied threats. I'd become a parent flying with a baby.

What's worse, after years as a single traveler I completely understood those looks when I boarded the plane—looks that pleaded with me to gate-check my baby. It was all I could do to keep from requesting to be seated away from myself.

So, for what it's worth, here's my advice for air travel in the first eighteen months of a baby's life: Skip it. For that first year and a half either make everyone come to you or get creative. Need to visit Grandma and Grandpa in Florida? Try teleconferencing. It's all the rage and so much more convenient for all involved. Tell your parents that the miracle of fiber optics allows for all the bonding with none of the smells or stains.

If that doesn't work, and the inheritance is riding on your getting baby Wentworth III some face time with Wentworth Sr., give serious thought to loading up the Buick and making the trek by land.

If you do opt to take to the open road by car, know this: Car trips with your baby are all about toys. Toys are your friends—even if it's a two-dollar fake cell phone that beeps and asks, "Operator. Can I connect you?" in a distinctly Taiwanese accent. A five-minute drive without a plastic distraction can lead to boredom. Boredom can lead to crying, which can lead to screaming, which can lead to me doing the same thing I do when I hear a funny noise coming from my car engine. I turn up the stereo.

On the upside, longer car trips with a baby can lead to some interesting discoveries. You know all those rest stops off the interstate that you always bypassed because you thought they were frequented solely by truckers and adventurous gay men? Well, you'll be investigating a lot of those with your baby. Babies need to make frequent stops to get out of the car and stretch their lungs. With any luck your baby's lungs will be loud enough to drown out the adventurous gay men.

But if due to circumstances beyond your control you absolutely can't avoid subjecting your cherub to the friendly skies, and vice versa, there is one piece of good news: I'm fairly certain that flying with babies is why God made it possible to get buzzed off one drink at high altitudes.

When I was finally forced to fly with my daughter, I may have set off some red flags by trying to order my first in-flight drink while in line for the metal detector. But by that point I had plenty of reason to be on edge.

Long before you face down the cold stares of an entire 767 filled with business travelers eyeing your infant like an eighteen-pound noise and strep factory, you have to cope with an even more terrifying specter: a playgroup full of helpful mommies needing to pass along their triumphant advice and stories about how they got little Joshua from Los Angeles to Houston like a little huggable Charles Lindbergh (if only BabyGap made eighty-five-dollar Li'l Aviator goggles . . .).

These mommies may tell you it's a good idea to schedule your flight for during your baby's nap time, but I wouldn't bother trying this. First of all, even if you have a baby who sleeps like clockwork, have you ever seen an airline's departure schedule that wasn't a complete work of fiction? And even if your flight did depart on time, the chances of your baby's nap schedule not being completely thrown off are slim to none. So, I say plan your trip at a time that's convenient for you, so that at least one of you isn't tired.

A few helpful frequent fliers preached the wonder of slipping your baby a little Benadryl about twenty minutes before takeoff, claiming it helps keep baby's ears clear and knocks him out cold, rendering him a cuddly carry-on for the duration of the flight. This advice *works like a charm*—for other people. My baby slept peacefully for the first five minutes, but as soon as sweet Mr. Benadryl kicked in, she was wired for sound—for the rest of the flight. Turns out there is a possible reverse reaction for some babies, causing them to be *more* active instead of less.

Too bad that helpful advice didn't come with a pharmaceutical-ad-style disclaimer, a rapid-speaking announcer who would tag the suggestion with the following: *In many cases Bendadryl may also act as a potent stimulant, triggering rampant hyperactivity and rendering the baby as manic as Robin Williams on a telethon . . . a five-hour telethon, stretching from coast to coast, that you cannot turn off.*

You may want to road test that Benadryl trick when you aren't trapped on a plane, because you're going to want that information *before* you're forty thousand feet up.

But take heart, there are things you can do to cut down on the agony. First off, buy your baby his or her own seat. Yes, I know it's a lot cheaper to just keep your kid in your lap, but holding a squirming baby in your lap for hours, especially on a packed plane, is not my idea of a great time. I understand that if you decide to hold your baby on your lap and the plane is not full, you can have the seat next to you for free, but is this a gamble you're willing to take? I'm not.

Preparation is half the battle. So know that your prep time will triple from what you're used to. If you are the type of person who likes to throw your stuff together two hours before departing for a cruise around the world, and who makes it to the airport with only moments to spare, maybe having a child wasn't your best lifestyle choice.

Do yourself a favor and get to the airport on the early side. And by "early side," I mean the night before. If you are leaving a car at the airport, make it two days before. One of the toughest parts of the trip will be lugging all your crap through the airport and getting through security. You'll have to fold up the stroller to put it through the X-ray machine, and then send the infant seat through without the baby in it. I'm surprised they actually let you carry your child through without making you put them on the belt. By the way, if you happen to set off the metal detector while holding your baby, they will actually pat your baby down as well. Although, this could actually be a good thing if you had had any suspicions about your baby being a terrorist but you hadn't wanted to come right out and accuse them.

When traveling with a toddler, if there is a problem with your ticket or boarding pass, try not to swear under your breath like you used to at the idiot behind the ticket counter, because your child will inevitably hear you and repeat it like a mantra: "Ash ho, ash ho, ash ho!" This will be the end of your upgrades to first class.

You'll want to overpack your carry-on. You really and truly can't have enough stuff with you. Pay special attention to food, diapers, and clothing changes. If you're

breast-feeding, you're all set, but if your baby is on formula, bring extra. You might want to pack a tub of
formula in case you get trapped somewhere overnight
with less than stellar accommodations, like, say, *the airport
terminal*. The gift shop is a little light on baby supplies,
although current issues of *Us Weekly* can double for baby
wipes in a pinch. Be warned, the "Celebrities, They're
Just Like Us" section may never seem quite the same.

On the plus side, I bet you're thinking that you will
finally get the chance to preboard legally. Not so fast.
You may want to do this with a tiny infant, but not with
an active baby or small child. It's just that much more
time for them to get whiny and realize the seat in front
of them is a good place for hard kicking.

You'll need to give your child something to suck on
when the plane is taking off and when it's landing. This
will counteract the pressurization and reduce the
chances of painful earaches. This will also mean fewer
passengers with painful earaches caused by your baby's
screaming, because it's tough to cry when there's a
nipple shoved in your mouth.

Bring activities for yourself, because you won't be
doing any sleeping. I for one would have to down a
bottle of NyQuil to fall asleep anywhere but in my
own bed, but even if you're a good airborne sleeper,
you'll find it rough to fall asleep on a plane with your
baby. With that in mind it's a good idea to lower your
viewing standards, because you'll need to watch the

in-flight entertainment, even if it's *Deuce Bigalow IV: Outer Space Gigolo*.

Of course, you'll need to bring a few things to entertain your baby. But even if you forget, don't worry, they'll find many things to amuse themselves with right on the plane. A bag of pretzels, the in-flight magazine (at least *someone* will be entertained by this thing), a plastic spoon, or an empty Stoli minibottle can be a great time for a baby. A rousing game of peekaboo with the person seated behind you is always a good time killer too, but I suggest putting a time limit on it, because after about twenty minutes it can get a little creepy.

The nice thing is, if you've ever had a problem with people in the seat next to you wanting to engage you in tedious conversation and to show you their entire collection of photos from the family reunion they just attended, if you're traveling with only your baby, you won't have that problem now! In fact, you may now find yourself on the receiving end of the old "Gosh, I'd love to assist, but this Danielle Steel novel is impossible to put down." Remember, this isn't a popularity contest. You're flying to reach your destination, not to make friends. Some people may actually like you, think your baby's cute, and even offer to help you carry things, and others will be annoyed no matter how great your baby acts. No one can fault you for doing your best. Babies cry; if people don't like it, tough titty. At least until I'm back to being a single flier, then the original rules apply once again.

Little Brainiacs

Why is it that whenever I see someone with one of those precious MY CHILD IS AN HONOR STUDENT AT SUCH AND SUCH ELEMENTARY SCHOOL bumper stickers I instantly want to key their car? It doesn't sweeten the pot that they're usually on a cell phone in a SUV bigger than Nell Carter, but that's a separate matter. There was a time when a bumper sticker like that meant a parent was proud of their progeny and wanted to notify the entire freeway! Now it's a depressing reminder that the obsession with raising Superkids has gotten way out of hand.

I met a woman at a party when I was pregnant, and with no foreplay she asked me which preschools I'd applied to so far. I said, "I'm only six months along!"

She sucked in a breath and said, "Ooooh, you probably missed the boat for a really good one. Well, at least you're talking to your baby, right? In a foreign language? And putting headphones on your stomach so the baby can listen to classical music? According to the studies there's a lot you can do now to raise your baby's IQ."

It was at that moment I started to miss binge drinking.

I tried so hard to block this stress out. I never went to any expensive private schools or had expensive educational toys, but I did have a mom who read to me every night without fail, so I figured my baby would be fine too. But it's almost impossible to avoid these education zealots. They're worse than Hare Krishnas—ready to pounce and handing out "well-meaning" advice in malls, grocery stores, parks, pretty much anywhere that people with children congregate. The pressure these days to make your baby smart is intense. That's why I recommend not leaving the house from the time you get knocked up to at least a year after giving birth. Make it two just to be safe. When you reemerge, you can pretend you had a bad bout of postpartum agoraphobia and that any ill-timed comment could send you right back to the great indoors.

I had really looked forward to the perks of being pregnant. You know, quitting my job, snacking nonstop, having men give up their seats on the bus for me. I know, that's obviously crazy talk; I would never ride the bus. But I thought pregnancy would at least be downtime while I got myself mentally prepared for the rigors of waking up every day before noon. I had no idea that I was supposed to be playing Chopin and teaching my embryo a foreign language. Hey, at this point *English* is a foreign language. Can't we let it get a grasp on that first?

Sorry, but no matter how much reading and talking

in Chinese you do to your belly, the baby is not going to pop out speaking Mandarin. Possibly Cantonese—but that's a much simpler language. If you're dying for your child to speak Chinese, why not adopt a *Chinese* kid? The upside is in a few years they can do your taxes. On the other hand, they'll cost you a bundle in car insurance.

If it's this bad when you're merely pregnant, I'm scared to think where this quest to make your child into a genius is going to go next—pre-conception? Are you going to play *Swan Lake* to your husband's sperm before he gets you pregnant, to get a jump on the competition? People have lost their minds. Leave your fetuses alone! They're not born yet! Maybe this will help you get the picture: Go to your OB's office and look closely at your ultrasound. See that? Your baby is smoking an itty-bitty cigarette to calm his itty-bitty nerves! You're going to have to get him an itty-bitty patch!

I'll tell you who the true geniuses are: the ones who came up with the Baby Einstein DVDs. These things are like heroin to new moms. You're a stronger person than I if you resisted the peer pressure to pick up a dozen of these bad boys. I love my baby with all my heart, and I would sooner go fishing with Scott Peterson than with-hold an opportunity for my child to reach her fullest potential and . . . AND THAT'S HOW THEY GET YOU! You guiltily hand over $19.99 to have a fuzzy felt puppet attempt to teach your three-month-old French! I have to say, watching a puppet in a raspberry beret speak with a bad French accent is downright frightening—unless you're buzzed, then it's hilarious—and yet I bought the boxed set. Let me be the first to tell you, they are pretty much all alike. You pull that cellophane off your newest find, hoping for something fresh and different, and it's just another day, another sock puppet.

But it doesn't matter. All the babies I know are addicted to them. My baby stared at them much the way I watch the audition episodes of *American Idol*—not quite understanding what I'm seeing yet riveted all the same. But the real reason I use them is not to teach my baby anything, it's so I can take a shower.

The main focus should be on toys your baby enjoys playing with, not toys that you hope will turn them into the next Bill Gates. Think about it, when your husband's playing Madden NFL 2006, is it because he wants to learn to coach football or because he wants to block out your bitching for a half hour?

Baby Einstein is only one of many product lines that claim to help your baby not turn out to be a dumbass. You can buy a CD-ROM called Brite Kids—yes, that's how they spell it (way to get off on the right foot)—as well as one called Brainy Baby, one called So Smart!, and one, I think, called Future Asshole!

Plus the "learning" toys are way too expensive. I challenge you to make it out of Babies "R" Us for any less than a hundred bucks. Don't get me wrong, I value my baby's toys. I want her to have things that stimulate her, but if your baby is anything like mine, she can burn two hours playing with a set of measuring cups, which are free—and in my case, still in the original packaging. When my daughter was nine months old, I succumbed to the pressure and spent forty dollars on one of those LeapFrog LeapStart Learning Tables that come complete with a keyboard, drum machine sounds, and other annoying noises. She would cruise right by it every time, opting instead for a remote control that had long ago stopped functioning for any electronic equipment in our house.

Before you know it, your personal tutoring time will be over, and it will be time to get your baby off to one of those prep preschools the zealots have been bitching to us about. There was a time when preschool meant (wink-wink) babysitting! Now our kids are supposed to graduate preschool magna cum laude, with earning potential.

That's provided they can get in. One preschool that I briefly considered had an arduous application process. I was given a ten-page application that asked questions like, "What are your child's strengths and weaknesses?"

"Hmm . . . one of her strengths is that she is a real 'people person.' And she's up early every morning! Let's see . . . her weaknesses are she's not really a 'team player,' and she tends to take things that don't belong to her . . . and chew on them."

But wait, I then found out there was an interview.

"What kind of interview?" I made the mistake of asking. I was told that my child would have to sit with one of the teachers and have a chat with her, and then my baby would be observed playing with other children, so that her maturity level could be assessed before she was considered as a candidate for that school. I chose to let the woman at the school know in a mature nonverbal way what I thought of her "interview process," by hanging up on her. Yeah. It turned out the twenty-five-dollar application fee was nonrefundable.

Can any child really be that much better off because they attended an exclusive (read "expensive") preschool? What exactly is being taught that's worth taking out a second mortgage on your house? Your kid is not going to earn an advanced degree in drawing a crayon outline of his hand. That doesn't come until college. Preschool is the time children should be learning life's basics: how to tie their shoes, how to fight the urge to bite people, and how to make a blended margarita—you know, usable skills. FYI, little guys, easy on the Triple Sec.

By the way, even in the more relaxed preschools, biting another child, which used to be a rite of passage, can now get your three-year-old suspended or booted out of school. Some kids have even been ordered to attend a two-hour anger management seminar. Oh wait, that was me.

It only gets worse when the children are ready to start elementary school. If you even *think* about sending your

kid to the dreaded public school, watch out, the education zealots will have some statistic at their disposal. One
opinionated neighbor I couldn't avoid let me know gleefully that six out of seven children who attend public
school will at some point be arrested for prostitution.
Okay, that doesn't sound 100 percent right, but my mind
was wandering a bit. Believe me, it's the only way to get
through a conversation with these types.

And let's not even suggest homeschooling as an
alternative to all this. You have to be in a completely
other gene pool to homeschool your children. Andrea
Yates homeschooled her kids. Next topic.

If the schoolwork doesn't kill your kid's spirit, the
extracurricular activities will. These poor bastards need a
Palm Pilot to keep up with their daily obligations: ballet,
tae kwon do, step aerobics, Young Republicans, and so
on. Some of them are putting in an eighty-hour work
week with no compensation. I know Mexican busboys
who put in fewer hours, and at least they get tips.

I don't want to burst anyone's bubble, but there's no
scientifically proven way to make your kid's IQ higher or
to make sure they get into the college of your choice.
Maybe this is a blessing. Personally, I don't want my
daughter being smarter than me. It doesn't look good for
her, and more important, it's embarrassing for me. Is there
anything more annoying than a four-year-old with better
grammar than her parents? If your kid is ordering for you
at a French restaurant, it's not adorable, it's disturbing.

No one likes precocious kids. Sure they're cute on sitcoms, but trust me, you don't want one in your own home. Think of your social life. Wouldn't you rather have your kid be tolerable at a dinner party than hyperventilating at a spelling bee? Fine, I'm the heavy. But I'm right about this. It's not just *your* social life that will suffer either. Momma's little high achiever is going to have a lot of alone time in junior high to think about how smart he is. Do you really want your kid to need roofies to get lucky? It's up to you.

Look on the "brite" side; smarts are not always necessary to get into a good college—George Dubya went to Yale, and I hear he *still* plays with measuring cups. And college is not absolutely necessary for your kid to have a decent career. But, you might be asking, "What if my baby wants to be a doctor?" Come on, a lot of that "medical" stuff is common sense. If you want them to be a doctor, have them watch *ER* religiously and get the lingo down. They can easily get a good feel for the job that way. Sure if they want to be a specialist they might need some schooling, but they can easily be a GP (that's general practitioner to the lay person). Helping your child reach her potential requires drive, commitment, and a lot of space on your TiVo.

Bottom line, this approach makes about as much sense as anything the folks at Baby Einstein have thought up. All I know is, if my baby wants to be a lawyer, we're in great shape. I watched a ton of *Law & Order* while I was pregnant.

Women Who Love Their Babies Too Much

You know those people whose outgoing voice mail message says something like: "Tammy, Nate, and little Baby oooh-so-huggable-cutie-cute-Kaitlin aren't here right now. Leave a message!" followed by a small child screeching for fifteen seconds?

If you're one of those people, you may want to save us both some pain and skip this chapter. Use the extra time to coordinate Li'l Kaitlin's BabyGap sweater sets, and meet the rest of us back at the next chapter. Go on now, get!

Okay, they're gone. Can the rest of us please agree: They must be stopped. I don't understand the logic. I want to leave a message for them that says "No one is leaving a message for your baby! Your baby doesn't have friends! And if you're leaving your baby's name on the voice mail to let me know you have a baby, *please don't!* If I don't know it by now, then I'm not someone who needs this information!"

I want to say this, but thanks to supreme willpower

and an old linty Valium I found in a drawer, I don't.

You've seen this mother when you're out of the house in the middle of the afternoon; the one who dresses herself and her kid in matching mommy-baby outfits, the one whose Internet screen name is TylersMommy, and whose license plate reads MOMOF4, and her key chain reads—you get the picture. This breed of mother craves the "Mommy" crown like Winona Ryder craves a free Fred Segal bag. They spend so much time focused on their kids that they couldn't pick their husband's penis out of a police lineup. This is Mommy Fever.

If you've ever been stuck talking to a woman in the throes of this affliction, you know it can be a near-death experience. When it comes to the topic of their children, without so much as a single espresso these mommies become the Energizer Bunny; they keep going and going and going and going. If you want to freak them out, try moving the subject away from their baby, and watch as their eyes glaze over and their brain leaves their body. They will even silently finger an imaginary picture of their baby until the bad conversation goes away.

Some are so hyperfocused on their baby that they will take it personally if "Little Joshy" doesn't react to them like a long-lost lover every single time. They will concoct endless scenarios for the lack of response. "He must be soooo tired." "Hmmm, I wonder if he has a fever." "I've never seen him act like this." Try saying, "Maybe he's just not that into you." It'll send them straight to the wine aisle every time.

There are some situations for which there is no defense. You may access your voice mail and find a message like this. *"Hi,* it's Tiffany's mommy [yes, some women gain a child and lose a name]. Tif and I were wondering if you want to meet us for lunch at around four o'clock. . . . Sorry so late, but Tiffany eats breakfast at seven, then has a nap at nine thirty. Oh, then we have mommy-baby quality playtime till twelve . . . snack . . . Gymboree at one . . . snack time . . . but if she doesn't get another nap in, she'll be so cranky. . . . You know what, better make it four thirty. . . . Oh, shoot, Tif and I have couple's therapy today. Let's definitely do it tomorrow. Unless she's teething . . ."

Obviously these mommies are incredibly annoying to their husbands, friends, and pretty much anyone who has to share space with them for more than five seconds, but to a new mother they can be downright lethal. You see, the übermommy disease is contagious. And in a new mom's fragile state it's all too easy to get sucked down the mommy rabbit hole and start to think this behavior is normal. It's like if you shop in the mall frequently, after a while four dollars for a cookie at Mrs. Fields seems about right.

If you're a new mom, of course you'll take tons of pictures of your baby, display them in every room of your house, and e-mail them to friends, distant acquaintances, and anyone whose e-mail address you possess. If you didn't, that would be weird. But if you become convinced that a life-size mural of your baby in the living room is not merely a fantastic idea but completely necessary and long overdue, you should take stock of your situation.

Do you and the women you spend time with begin and end every conversation with "As a mom . . ."? Do you have a Web site devoted to your toddler? Do you update that Web site no fewer than eighteen times a day? If this strikes you as acceptable behavior, consider this an intervention.

All new moms are hardwired to feel overprotective and attached to their babies, especially when the babies are newborns. Parents of newborns are known to nudge their fragile sleeping babies awake, just to be positive that the baby is breathing. I, myself, often had trouble resisting the urge to do this, but at a certain point it's no longer okay. You have to learn healthy boundaries.

When my baby was around eight months old, I used to kind of miss her when she was sleeping. One night around eleven I wandered into her room as I often did. I stood over her crib and watched her take her little sweet baby breaths. I started thinking, *Ooh, I want to wake her up just for a minute. I don't think I can wait until tomorrow to say hi and see her cute smile. Besides, she'll get a kick out of seeing me, too!* But I *didn't*—because she was *sleeping! And that would be wrong!* Instead I decided to wake up my husband. As you can imagine, he got pretty pissed, and as an adult he had no problem finding the four-letter words to express his feelings. Later, as I lay on the couch alone with my thoughts, I internalized the invaluable lesson I'd learned that night: *Every maternal, nurturing, and well-meaning impulse that crosses your synapses should not necessarily be acted upon.* That, and no more coffee after nine p.m.

The logic that leads some mommies to take their kids with them everywhere usually follows this line: They assume their child wouldn't be able to tolerate being without them, they can't imagine any situation where a baby wouldn't be invited, and they are trying desperately to make up for a lack of adult companionship. Please stop.

Although a hormonal übermom is often resistant to reason, I offer these counterpoints: (1) Your child needs to be away from you sometimes. It's good for them. You're not that fascinating. Let them miss you. (2) There are plenty of places where babies and kids are not welcome—that's what is so great about being an adult. (3) There is no substitute for adult companionship. If you spend too much time with your baby, other adults will eventually lose interest in spending time with you. Adults have expectations of other adults. Like that they refrain from speaking baby talk in a restaurant.

The bottom line is, being married to your baby isn't going to work out well for anyone involved. First off, babies don't make good husbands. They're too young to get into R-rated movies, they're rarely up for a good political debate, and they couldn't connect a DSL line if their little lives depended on it. And, mommies, as much as you mean well, you aren't doing your babies any favors by making them your whole life. You are only creating little narcissistic monsters who will never be able to tolerate any of life's little disappointments. Insurance won't cover an extended stay at Bellevue over the cancellation of *Rugrats*. Believe me, I've checked.

Remember, many children who are overprotected, are overly doted on, or are extensions of their mommies become serial killers—or worse, reality TV stars. I have a feeling that Charles Manson's mother had a license plate that said LILCHARLIESMOMMY! So please, get a hobby. The child you save may be your own.

Birthday Parties and Other Events I Don't Want to Be Invited To

At the end of the first year of parenthood a lot of parents are tempted to throw their infant a fancy birthday bash. Please don't. I completely understand the urge, but it is a waste of time and money to go to great lengths for someone who thinks a big night is some alone time with your Tupperware. *You're* the one who needs to be congratulated on surviving the first year of parenthood with your sanity and marriage intact. But your baby can't distinguish this day from any other.

Unfathomably, there are people out there who go crazy with the celebrating, spending more money on their baby's first birthday than an NBA player spends on child support. While standing in line at McDonald's (one underappreciated baby perk is you will now be waking up before McDonald's stops serving breakfast), I heard a woman talking loudly on her cell phone. She was saying something to the effect of "Ralph and I are throwing Julianna a huge party for her first birthday. Our catering budget alone is eight thousand dollars."

My first thought was, *If you have eight grand to spend on food, why on Earth are you eating at McDonald's?* My next thought was, *Eight thousand dollars just for the food?* I mean, their little tulip is only a year old! I seriously doubt she could even tell the difference between osetra and beluga caviar. Plus if this woman was forking out eight grand on only the food, what was she planning for the entertainment? Was she going to have Captain Kangaroo dug up and reanimated for a personal appearance at her daughter's bash? I was so irritated I could barely finish my second McGriddle.

These are the same people who invite you to their kid's graduation from preschool, their ballet recital, baptism, first pedicure, tarot card reading, or anything else that Hallmark makes a card for. The ironic part is, if I did receive an invitation to an over-the-top birthday gathering for a one-year-old, the only possible way it would be tolerable is if there were no one-year-olds in attendance.

Let's be logical here. What is the point, really, of making a big deal out of your twelve-month-old's birthday? Do we think they're going to spend the day reflecting on the crazy year they've had? Looking back fondly on when they took their initial swig of apple juice, rolled over for the first time, and learned to *almost* say the word "bird"—not the whole word, just the *B* sound?

I don't think so. They're going to do what they do the other 364 days of the year: watch a video, throw food on the floor, have a nap, gnaw on something they're not supposed to, cry, and repeat.

The first couple of years, when your child is blissfully unaware of their birthday, should really be thought of as free years. Why pull out all the stops while your baby has no long-term memory anyway? Besides which, your baby will probably only be scared by all the excess fuss and attention, and you will spend your quality drinking time comforting them. A good rule of thumb is no birthday party until they can say "birthday party."

The time will come soon enough when you'll need to celebrate your kid's big day in style—complete with Gucci goody bags, moon bouncers, and creepy clowns. You don't want to burn out in the first couple of years. If you do, by the time they get to the age of five, you'll be done, and they'll just be getting started.

Don't kid yourself, birthday parties have become an institution with a high probability of determining your child's social standing—much the way our brand of jeans determined ours. A pair of knockoff Jordache jeans ruined my junior high cred for a full two years. I still think if my mom had splurged on one pair of Calvins, I might've lost my virginity before the age of twenty.

As unwelcome as it may be, you'll be saddled with some responsibility over your kid's popularity. Their party has to be as good as their best friend's party, regardless of how much nondisposable income it takes to make this happen. You'll have to stock goody bags with treats for the entire class roster of kids who're invited, come up with a fun and creative place to hold it, and make sure that everyone has the time of their fifth-grade life. It's a lot of pressure. So why not pace yourself and throw them a good one in a couple of years when it will actually matter?

Regardless of what I say, some people won't be able to resist the urge to throw some type of first birthday party, and luckily for them, there is a whole industry built around it. Spend three minutes on the Internet and you'll find endless places to buy swag for all your popular birthday themes, such as Barney, *Bear in the Big Blue House*, and *Sesame Street*. I looked for *Dog the Bounty Hunter*, but, strangely, couldn't find it anywhere, so if you're sold on this trendy theme, you may have to make it yourself.

You can also find suggestions for activities and games for the big event. I found one Web site that promises "Bright Ideas for Busy Families." This site, AmazingMoms.com, says that "realistically, one-year-old parties are for the grown-ups to celebrate," and then they offer up some game ideas that adults can enjoy. There's one called Baby's First Guessing Game, where, in a nutshell, you're supposed to collect photos or hand-drawn pictures as mementos of big firsts in your baby's life, such as her first smile. Then you're supposed to tack these mementos up on the wall and let all of your guests take a stab at guessing when the events happened.

Whoever gets the most right wins a prize! Or how about one called Baby Bottle Bowling, where you fill ten baby bottles with water or rice, arrange them like bowling pins, and let people take turns throwing a ball to either get a strike or break a lamp.

By the looks of the planning and the attention span it would require to put these games together, the AmazingMoms.com Webmaster and I have very different definitions of the word "busy." If you want to try any of these games, I'd suggest getting started while your baby's still gestating.

Why go through that much trouble when with a little imagination you can play some clever games that are practically ready to go! I've come up with a couple of party games for *truly* busy families; the games are also, surprisingly, time-savers.

Here's a game I call Laundry Relay that's *loads* of fun for all of your partygoers!

Set up two huge baskets of your clean but unfolded laundry. Separate your guests into two teams. Have each team run over to a basket of clothes and start folding! Whichever team can fold their basket of laundry first, wins.

Another game that's good clean fun is one I call the Unload the Dishwasher Race. This one is similar to the last one in that it's a race. First separate your guests into two teams, and then sit back and relax while you time the first team unloading the top level of the dishwasher, and then time the other team unloading the bottom. Whichever team finishes in the fastest time (without breaking anything) wins a glass of wine. Preferably from a nice bottle of pinot noir they were kind enough to bring over themselves.

Seriously, you're the one who's celebrating. So cut the charade that it's all for your baby, and if you must have a party, throw a nice casual cocktail party for after the baby's already put down to bed for the night If you want to, you can give your baby a little cupcake and sing "Happy Birthday," and then off to bed we go!

Perhaps at the end of the evening you can even give out goody bags for your adult guests. May I suggest a light porno DVD, a split of Moët, and a few condoms? Your guests will definitely go home happy.

When my daughter turned one, we chose to keep it really simple. My husband and I did a shot of tequila, high-fived each other, and called it a year. Hell, we were tired. Granted, she'll be traumatized when she realizes her first birthday passed with no pomp and circumstance, but I'm confident that eventually, with the guidance of a good therapist and a lot of intense journaling, she'll be able to work through it and keep her self-esteem intact.

If this is a worry for you, you have my permission to go ahead and tell your kid they had a huge birthday party. How are they going to know any different? With modern technology you can cut and paste your little boy's or girl's picture into another kid's party pictures, whose parents went all out and threw an expensive bash. It's pretty simple, really: People who care about their children have Adobe Photoshop.

And as far as presents go, less is more here, too. I have a feeling your one-year-old will be way more thrilled with a plastic Folgers instant coffee container lid than any gift that comes from Bloomingdale's. And, bonus, you won't even need a gift receipt.

Name Calling

Why is it suddenly cool to give your kids ridiculous names? When you're expecting a baby, one of the cherished rites is sitting around and trying to pick out a name that your bump will someday call his own. It's one of the few productive things you can do while you're pregnant to prepare for your baby's arrival, that doesn't involve heavy lifting—other than eating an entire Pillsbury refrigerated chocolate chip cookie dough roll.

Unfortunately, naming your baby can be overwhelming. After all, this is going to be your child's identity for life, providing they don't become an actor, stripper, or mob informant. The chosen name may in fact be a strong determining factor in their future endeavors. I defy you to find me one person named Cherries Jubilee who wasn't destined to go into porn.

In choosing a moniker for your child you have to look at it as a lifelong investment and, as such, approach it with a fine balance of creativity, foresight, and compassion. Sadly, the equation seems to have fallen alarmingly out of whack of late.

One major culprit, the same people who introduced us to Ugg boots and lips filled with ass fat: celebrities. Flip open any *People* magazine, or, if you're really shameless, pull out the *In Touch Weekly*. You'll find it's a parade of Dakotas, Rumors, Dylans, Cinnamons, and Tallulahs. But just because celebrities do it doesn't mean you can get away with naming your little ruby-cheeked cherub "Apple." Trust me, celebrity spawn are hothouse flowers, nurtured in special schools with other celebrity seedlings, who more than likely also sport ludicrous names. No one will let on that names like Tiger Lily and Prince Michael are freakish, until they're in the adult world, where people will usually be too polite to openly snicker past the bodyguard.

Your child, however, will not be extended this same privilege and, given a name like Minerva or Fauntleroy, will be subjected to countless acts of brutality between kindergarten and community college. If you still don't believe me, talk to anyone named Moon Unit who *isn't* related to Frank Zappa.

But in the swoon of pregnancy the brutality of the school yard seems far removed. Believe me, I know. I was on such a third trimester high that my daughter came *this close* to a life spent answering to "Winter." In that spirit let me help your process along by giving you a few guidelines to steel you while you're perusing the *Names That Will Ensure Your Child Stays a Virgin Until They're Thirty* book.

Cutesy Names—Skyy, Ashlynn, BreAnna, Mykalyn, Mackenzie. If you go with anything from this palette, know that you are most likely a latent pageant mom. A handle like this will almost ensure that your kid will be entering a Miss Junior Supreme Dazzle Queen or Li'l Mister Debonair Junior King contest by the age of six months. Best to shy away from these unless you live in Sugar Land, Texas, and pageants are your goal.

Spelling—When it comes to spelling, less is more. Lisa is a nice name. Lyssah, on the other hand, is about as distinctive as a homemade tattoo. And try to spell your chosen name within the same school district of how it sounds. There's nothing more aggravating for your child than having to repeatedly spell her name for someone, often the elementary-school sub, who is getting increasingly irritated with her. It's not her fault that you spelled the name Angela *A-y-n-g-y-l-l a.*

Legacy Names—Many names are handed down out of family tradition. As such, these names often carry more meaning and are an excellent way to honor generations past, but don't go nuts. Heavyweight boxer George Foreman named all five of his sons George. Yes, really. I think after scribbling "George" on a third birth certificate you really need to start asking yourself some hard questions, such as, "Why can't I come up with even one other name?" "How long can I outrun the Census Bureau?" and "Should I have left the boxing ring before age fifty-two?" Let's go ahead and cap the juniors at one.

Old-Fashioned Names—When considering an old-fashioned name, keep the century in mind. Several decades old is kitschy, such as Ruby or Gretchen; a hundred years, and we're getting into some unpleasant territory. No one wants to grow up with the name Hildegard anymore, and the same goes for Gladys, Gertrude, Ethel, Mildred, Edith, Beulah, or Maude. These names had their day, now it's time to let them go.

Product Names—A momentary salute to the maker of the top-shelf champagne, Cristal, is not worth condemning your daughter to a career in Lucite heels. Ditto your warm sentiments toward your Mercedes, bottled-water brand, or rum. Hey, I like Captain Morgan as much as the next gal, but I'd never date one.

Rhyming or Alliterative Names—I've always suspected that families who select their children's names to all begin with the same letter might be manifesting a form of OCD. And, this being a genetic disorder, I'd recommend laying out some meds for Kelly, Kendall, and Kristen. I know it's a common practice, but it can't help but make your kids feel like part of a matched set, and somehow incomplete on their own. If you bore offspring only to name them Irene and Eileen, or Brad, Chad, and Tad, you really should have collected Hummel figurines instead.

Popular Names—Just to let you know, I think we're good on Brandons, Ryans, Tylers, Dylans, Zacharys, Madisons, Hannahs, Emilys, Ashleys, Kaitlans, and Zoeys. We've reached our quota of names people picked from watching Fox and The WB. There's a memo going out to all expectant moms telling them the news, so if I were you, I'd have a backup name ready at the hospital in case they don't allow your first pick.

Let's put our heads together and give some serious thought to starting up new name trends. Because at this point we need to either come up with some different names altogether or come full circle back to Michael, David, Jennifer, and Mary.

Whatever you decide, make that decision with care and don't feel shy about focus-grouping with some trusted advisors. I know you don't want to tell anyone your choice for fear of being talked out of it, but you're hormonal right now, and maybe it's not best that you're given free rein. Remember what we've discussed: No more fruits, vegetables, states, days, or months. We need to get back to names that people can pronounce, that are spelled correctly, and that above all are not Coco. Come on, Courtney, that's why God created cats.

Much Ado About Doo

A friend of mine once went to a dinner party with her very new boyfriend. The couple throwing the party had a three-year-old son who was getting potty trained, and when my friend walked into their house, she was greeted by a little boy and the words "I poop." It seemed their tyke had had his first major success! There was much elation in the house, and my friend was immediately whisked into the kid's father's office, where she was subjected to pictures of his son on the toilet *and* a close-up digital photo of the product of the monumental event. Let's just say, my friend lost her appetite for dinner, and her new boyfriend didn't get lucky that night. But at least she wasn't sent home with a souvenir.

I know toilet training is a big milestone. I know you're excited. But no matter how proud you are the first time little Max takes a poop in the potty, seriously, do not have yourself videotaped next to the poop as though you'd just caught a huge bass, and don't save it in your scrapbook or display it as a centerpiece on your dining room table. This is not good form.

Toilet training is a big-deal part of parenting, and because of the challenging nature of teaching a child to use the potty, the process can get very competitive. Look over the bookshelves and you will find books to get you ahead in the potty game, such as *Potty Train in Three Days* and *Toilet Training in Less Than a Day*. I'm waiting for *Why Wait? Potty Training in Utero!*

Then, like it's not enough to be the fastest toilet trainer in the West, there are the parents who are attempting to train way too soon.

An article in *Newsweek* magazine[1] told about a mom in New York City, who started toilet training her son at *three weeks old*. According to the article she'd hold the little guy over the toilet when she thought he needed to go. She claimed that by the time her kid was nine months old, he could let her know when he had to go to the bathroom. Sure. And Clay Aiken's straight.

Look, even if the kid could indicate his bathroom needs (which really probably means he got that little grunt face that we all recognize), he can't walk himself over there, so that left her to bring an eighteen-pound pooping, peeing baby to the bucket twenty times a day and night. I'll just stick with the diapers for a while, thanks.

---

1. "Parenting: Ditching Diapers," MSNBC. http://www.msnbc.msn.com/id/9375368/site/newsweek/ (accessed Oct. 5, 2005).

This article went on to say the toilet training phenom "is part of a growing movement called 'infant potty training'—whose followers believe that most parents are overly reliant on diapers." She has followers? She holds her kid over a bucket when he's three weeks old, calls it a movement, and suddenly she's the Dalai Lama of potty training? Why is it that the people with the craziest ideas are always the first ones who want to take them public?

Most reasonably sane people begin toilet training when their child is somewhere between eighteen months and three years, and finish . . . sometime much, much later. Let's face it. Sadly, not everyone reading this book is *entirely* toilet trained. You're going to do a bunch of different things, some suggested by books or experts and some that you make up as you go along. But it doesn't help to go overboard on any particular technique. Like everything else in parenting, there's no magic formula, just a lot of patience.

To help get the little ones into the spirit of the process, there are fun books to read and helpful videos to watch. Why not sip a juice box and pop in the DVD *Potty Power* or sit on the commode and peruse *Time to Pee!* or *Once Upon a Potty?* Although, please don't read *Everyone Poops.* I think this book is highly misleading—at least for our little girls, 'cause if you're anything like me, you don't poop nearly enough. I think we need to teach our children that pooping is a luxury not a right. But don't worry, I'm not taking to the streets to start any movements ("Hell, no, I can't go!"). So, not everybody poops. Mommy doesn't.

"Toilet modeling" is another tactic the experts recommend for getting your child interested in the potty. This is where you show your child what it looks like when Mom and Dad sit on the toilet. If you are going to go the toilet modeling route, don't do it at Denny's. Been there, done that. Got myself Grand Slammed right out the door. Try it in the privacy of your own home and make sure your child is an active participant. If you're a little shy, they can give you lots of encouragement, yelling out things such as, "All right! Work it, Mom! Beautiful! Like that! Really sell it! Make me believe you're peeing! Now give me a little grunt!"

Okay, I just creeped myself out, which is tough to do.

When you get really deep into the potty training, some "authorities" on the subject advocate toting your baby's little potty around town with you. I'm sure this can be a lifesaver when you need to make an impromptu pit stop on the side of the road or when you find the "tiny people" accommodations lacking at a friend's house, but don't whip that thing out in Starbucks or the mall. And if you do squat your kid down in the middle of the purse section at Macy's, please, please don't ever ask me to hold it for you.

Persistence is key. Eventually you will have tried everything, including rewards, elaborate flushing rituals, and food coloring in the toilet bowl. No matter what, when, where, and how you do it, you are bound to hit a snafu. Please remember that when you're having trouble getting your little leaker potty trained, one thing that definitely doesn't help is trying to guilt them. This is best left to the experts—Jewish grandmas.

I was sitting in a mall bathroom stall one time (I know, my first mistake), when I heard a woman chastising her son, "No, you are not allowed to wash your hands! Little boys who can't hold their own penis and wee wee in the toilet are not allowed to wash their own hands." First off, this is not positive reinforcement. Shaming will not get the results you're after. Plus, when have you ever heard of a child *wanting* to wash his hands after peeing? That is a good impulse! I'd let him run with that if I were you.

As with every other aspect of parenting, serenity is your friend. If you are too stressed out about it, your kid will sense that and become stressed out too. This will only lead to accidents and tears (yours). Bottom line, relax. Your kid *will* eventually get potty trained. And sooner or later we'll all be back in diapers anyway.

Ain't Misbehaving

About two months before I was due to give birth, I spent an afternoon with a college friend of my husband's and her eighteen-month-old daughter, Jasmine. With my inexperience I thought it might be good practice to be around a baby so I could get an idea of how they work. Two hours with this tyke and I was completely freaked out. The kid screamed incessantly for anything she wanted. Not yelling—yelling would've been a pleasure—but full-pitched screaming. Then there was the hitting her mom in the face. Repeatedly. With each blow her mother would chastise her in a singsongy voice, "Jaaasmine, honey, please don't hit Mommy in the face. Mommy doesn't like that." Another smack. "Jazzzz . . . sweetie, I already told you forty times." BAM! "Honey, please don't do that anymore."

I can see "Please pass the maple syrup," but *"Please stop punching Mommy in the face"*? Isn't this polite request too understated for a toddler to really understand?

I came home that day poised to find potential

adoptive parents for our baby, but my husband, always the logical one, thought that was a bit extreme. He convinced me that having unpleasant children can be blamed at least 50 percent on parenting.

Brattiness. It's our biggest fear as new parents and half the reason we lightly skim through so many parenting books. We want to raise our children right. We want them to be empathetic, loving, creative, and respectful human beings who, through our patience, nurturing, and exemplary parenting skills, grow up to give something back to the world. Or at least we want them to stay out of the pokey. Unfortunately, these days, in trying to make up for the strictness of our parents, we can go overboard trying to be "understanding," and accidentally raise future stars of *Nanny 911*.

What's up with the parents who think it's charming when their youngster starts a fire in a restaurant kitchen or the parents who refuse to acknowledge there's a problem when Little Snugglepuss bites fourteen kids in preschool? Thirteen, sure, maybe they're experimenting, but there has to be a cutoff point. Furthermore, if your toddler has gone after another child's scalp with a staple gun, he's not "expressing himself"—he's a bad seed. Children with no boundaries, who don't hear the word no, quickly become the reason we, their parents, are not invited to cool social functions anymore.

My good friends had a party not too long ago where one couple's seemingly innocuous two-year-old son almost irreparably damaged the couple's friendship with the hosts. This little boy, let's call him Damien, spent his first fifteen minutes of the party testing the furniture's durability by jumping on it with muddy feet. Later he shoved both grubby paws into the hors d'oeuvres one after the other, ruining them for the rest of the guests. For an encore he sprinted around the house rubbing guacamole and other foods that didn't go with the color scheme into my friends' walls and newly upholstered white couch. My friends looked around in vain for the little demon's oblivious parents. But when they finally tracked the parents down, instead of putting an end to Damien's reign of terror, they cheered him on with shouts of "Look at you! Yay! You're so funny!" If they think this is funny, they're in for a real treat when Damien lights their house on fire.

By the way, the couple who hosted the party remain child-free to this day.

Look, I know kids aren't always going to be well behaved. That's a given. Most toddlers are going to poke other kids in the eye when you turn around, talk back to you, and have meltdowns in every section of Wal-Mart. Teary tantrums may be beyond your control, but complete obliviousness to your kid's bad behavior is not. And if your kid ruins your friend's couch, it's not cause for celebration. It's cause for picking up their dry-cleaning bill.

On the other hand, let's not take it too far. If your perfectly behaved Stepford Kids never dare get out of line, it might be because they're scared of you, and that's not commendable, that's disturbing. Don't get carried away with the discipline or you will end up with an obedient child in need of expensive therapy. The *Focus on the Family* guy, James Dobson, advocates spanking your children at the tender age of one. What is he spanking them with, his crack pipe? Please don't even think about doing this. Your twelve-month-old isn't misbehaving on purpose.

By the way, Mr. Dobson might want to stay out of Canada if he doesn't want to get arrested. In Canada it's against the law to apply corporal punishment to a child younger than eighteen months. Yet another reason besides Moosehead beer, nationalized heath care, and Mike Myers to love our neighbors to the north!

I'm in favor of discipline. I gave my daughter a time-out in the womb for kicking too hard. But obviously, I wasn't going to spank her. One, it's too harsh, and two, I couldn't reach. It's all about finding some middle ground. Start by letting kids know that their bad behavior will surely and consistently have consequences—be it a two-minute time-out or no pie for a month. Learn to say no with authority. If your child is kicking you in the leg and you tell her to stop but she keeps doing it, and then the phone rings and you decide it's easier to just ignore the kicking, your kid might mistakenly get the idea that kicking you in the leg is a perfectly acceptable way to burn off an afternoon. Soon she'll be enjoying this activity using your friends, relatives, and the guy next door with the gun collection and anger issues. So say no and mean no.

Also, don't try to reason with a toddler. A two-year-old doesn't need to understand the intricacies of why it's not a good idea to try to pry another kid's ear off at the base. He needs to know that it hurts the other child, and if he does it again, his dad's going to do something to him he won't like.

For the sake of innocent people who are forced to sit next to you and your child on an airplane, anyone trying to enjoy dinner in the same restaurant, and basically the general population, please learn to control your children. Make yourself aware of the signs that your child may be a little monster. Trust me, you are always the last to know.

Signs Your Child May Be Putting a Damper on Your Social Life

Every once in a while someone slips and "accidentally" refers to your child as a malignant spirit.

There isn't a babysitter within three states who will work for you.

The last person who visited your house had a warrant.

You've aged ten years in the past two.

Your kid's done something to your dog that required stitches.

Your kid's done something to you that required major surgery.

Your four-year-old swears more than a sailor with Tourette's.

You sleep with a Taser under your bed.

Your neighbors built an electric fence around their yard, and they don't have a dog.

Your four-year-old's picture is up at the post office.

Your kid's the official mascot for the Hells Angels.

X-treme Parenting

So by this point you may be thinking you've got a toehold on new motherhood. You've got the gear, have leads on three sitters without a visible body piercing among them, and possess a strategy that you're sure will make your shorty sleep like she just came off a three-day Vegas bender. Smooth sailing until puberty, right? Not so fast. According to a growing field of child-raising gurus, your boutique approach to parenting is *totally* 1990s. According to these Minivan Maharishis, the path to enlightened parenting demands that you adhere to an overall parenting philosophy.

These overall parenting philosophies (let's call them OPPs) are a lot like fad diets. They all claim to be the one true way to a healthy, happy baby, and they all claim that they can't work their magic unless you follow them to the letter. From the tough infant love of the Babywise method to the mawkish Attachment Parenting (known as AP in the biz), there is always some loopy parenting sage telling you that your kids will suffer if you don't do the philosophy exactly "right" or if you dare to stray from their odd and often draconian guidelines.

Of course, new mothers are sitting ducks for these parenting cults, because no one is more vulnerable than a new mom grasping for answers to questions that have no definite answers. We may never know for sure how much handling and stimulation a baby needs, how much crying is okay, or how to get the little buggers to sleep, but that doesn't stop these parenting prophets from claiming they have the answers to those dilemmas.

The tricky part is that some of these philosophies can actually start off with commonsense notions about how to nurture your child. But soon enough the good intentions are left in the dust. With OPPs a little of a good thing is never enough, and, among wide-eyed disciples, dissent is never tolerated.

A good example of how an OPP can take on a life of its own involves Attachment Parenting, one of the more widespread philosophies. AP is well meaning and very popular. My first experience with an AP parent was when I bumped into one in a baby store. Literally. My big old pregnant belly actually crashed into a woman shopping. This lady had a child of at least two and a half cradled in a sling across her chest, almost as if she had a thirty-six-pound broken arm in a Garanimals cast. I asked her out of curiosity what type of sling she was wearing. (I'd been given a Maya Wrap as a gift, which actually needed its own DVD so you could figure out how to use it.) She told me the name of the sling and added "It's recommended for AP parents." I stared at her blankly.

A friend was with me and acted as though she knew what the woman was talking about, so I made a split-second decision to not bring attention to my potential lack of parenting skills and just go with it. The woman explained with a smug smile that her daughter would let her know when she wanted to be put down. I was horrified. "What if that's not till she's a sophomore in college?" I accidentally wondered out loud. That cut short our lesson on AP.

Needing to find out if Attachment Parenting was something this woman had just picked up watching Animal Planet, I went home and immediately did some research on this mysterious parental approach. It turns out that a lot of these AP people do something called "baby wearing." Baby wearing means carrying your baby around in a sling for most of its sleeping and waking hours. I'm sorry, but if you're holding your baby 24/7, that's not a baby, that's a tumor. I couldn't help but think maybe this was a philosophy for those poor people who just don't have any furniture.

I learned more as I read on. The main elements of Attachment Parenting are: extended breast-feeding, cosleeping, and carrying or being with babies (especially newborns) every hour of the day. It read less like a parenting strategy than an invitation to a lifetime of codependence.

Once I became aware of the AP devotees, I was able to spot one at sixty paces: The mom asking at Babies "R" Us if they make cosleep bassinets that go up to eighty pounds. The telltale sling tan lines in summer, and of course, the breast-feeding six-year-old. I also noticed that hard-core AP followers aren't shy about offering advice to total strangers, evangelizing about breast-feeding at the drop of a hat, or condemning the evil of strollers. Maybe some understanding is warranted. After all, how much sleep are these zombies getting with their kids in the same bed with them from birth through junior high? At the core of this all is the idea that kids need a lot of nurturing. What could be more well intended than that? But when famed author and AP advocate Alice Miller claims that Nazi Germany was the result of Hitler's parents' failure to let him sleep in the family bed, I remember why I avoid these people.

AP is a great example of a parenting style that many well-meaning people have distorted until it's some kind of torture for parents, all in the name of "following the rules." If you actually look at Dr. William Sears's Web site, the philosophy plainly says that "AP is an approach, rather than a strict set of rules."[2] But, hey, why listen to him? He's only the guy who invented it.

Maybe Attachment Parenting sounds a little too soft and fuzzy for you? Then you might be a candidate for the opposite end of the OPP spectrum: The RIE parenting

2. http://www.askdrsears.com/html/10/T130300.asp.

technique. RIE stands for Resources for Infant Educarers. Yes, edu*carers*. They went and stuck the crazy right in the name!

The idea behind RIE is that parents should develop respectful relationships with their babies. RIE adherents believe that rather than teaching your child to grow by pushing him into structured activities and performance-oriented situations, parents should stay out of the way and trust that their baby can learn more by exploring on his own. Sounds good so far, right? But you may want to hold off until you read the fine print.

The RIE "educarer" shows respect by never picking up an infant without making a formal announcement to him beforehand, and then waiting for the child's permission. RIE parents are taught that putting a child in a swing isn't "respecting" them. The same goes for an activity center, a high chair, or any other restrictive device. Oh yeah, and you must feed your child on your lap until they're old enough to decide for *themselves* that sitting in a high chair is pretty darn convenient.

I know my baby laughs like a nut job when she's in a swing. But according to the RIE view, that's her way of letting me know that it horrifies her. If RIE is to be believed, I should now reexamine all the things that cause her to laugh or giggle, as they may be scarring her for life. Before you plunk down upward of thirty dollars a class, you should know that tickling may as well be a war crime to this crowd, and forget about windup toys. Thanks, RIE!

Hard-core RIE followers love to chastise. If you find yourself in close proximity to a gathering of RIE parents, you're likely to hear a curt "That's *not* RIE" snapped at any perceived transgression. (But then, if you stay away, you'll be out of earshot.) One RIE parent said to me, "Once you start doing RIE, it will be difficult to hang out with other parents who aren't doing RIE." Not to worry, we're more afraid of you than you are of us!

The Babywise method is another widespread OPP, and it is among the most controversial. This approach seems to have been created by control freaks and Palm Pilot fans. In a nutshell, Babywise teaches that you need to strictly dictate your baby's sleep and eating patterns, no matter what his reaction or mood. This clock-watching plan urges parents to close their eyes and plug their ears if a baby cries for food or refuses to sleep at six p.m. They fail to mention that if you don't pay attention to your baby's cues, you may end up with a baby who is badly dehydrated or who loses more weight than Nicole Richie.

Not long ago the RIE and Babywise methods marked the outer limits of overall parenting philosophies. But, like diets, new OPPs keep cropping up, and, unless they're more extreme than the one before, they'll never land their leader on *Oprah*. For my money, the current lunatic fringe in parenting is TCS. TCS stands for taking children seriously. It's a parenting philosophy that believes children should *never* be coerced to do *anything*.

If you and your child have a disagreement, you aren't even allowed to compromise! Two-year-old Cody wants to gnaw on Grandpa's assault bayonet from the war? He'll get no argument from a TCS mom! I guess the logic is that plastic surgery can rebuild his lower face, but the scar of being told no can never heal.

One other word of caution: The extremism isn't just for infants and toddlers. OPP grads now have alternative education philosophies as well. Of course, from magnet schools to Montessori there has always been a healthy range of education options for kids. But just as common-sense parenting has been under siege from the OPP movement, so too has the early-education system. Exhibit A: Waldorf schools, of which there are more than eight hundred around the country. They teach according to the rules of anthroposophy, which holds that the human being is fundamentally a spiritual being and that all human beings deserve respect as the embodiment of their spiritual nature. Sounds nice and harmless, sort of like something printed on the hemp reusable bags at the organic market. Well, Waldorfers also believe children should not be taught to read before they're eight years old, fairies are real, and children should never be allowed to color with a black crayon. It may all be well meaning, but I'm keeping my eye on them just in case.

Are you confused yet? Don't be. You don't need a class, religion, or philosophy to teach you how to love your child. If you want to hold your baby, hold your baby. If you want to put your baby down for a nap and she cries a little, so what? She'll stop. If your baby is hungry, feed her. *You* know what's best. You don't need to be given one strict way of doing things.

Can you trust the latest parenting philosophies anyway, when they come in and out of style quicker than bell-bottoms? One day letting your kid stick his finger in a light socket is repackaged as "a healthy exploration of his environment," and the next day that's totally outmoded and you must childproof your home until it resembles a padded cell—or expect to be reported to the local authorities. Tomorrow letting your kid cry a bit will help them learn to be more self-reliant, and the next day a mere moment of physical separation or crying will eventually ensure a more public breakdown than Margot Kidder's.

What we need is some good old-fashioned balance. If you trust your own instincts, you will learn to be responsive to your baby. You will know when to say yes and when to say no, and you will have the wisdom to say yes to yourself when you need to put the baby down and ask for some help. You'll have the insight to know when it's worth sixty bucks to have someone else come over and scrub your bathroom.

Balanced Parents know when to let their babies cry and when not to. Balanced Parents know when it's okay for a child to crawl into their bed, and when they need the bed all to themselves. Balanced Parents know when they need a break, and they have a couple of babysitters on speed-dial. Balanced Parents know when breast-feeding is achievable and when to let it go. Balanced Parents know when to pick up their baby, and when to let their baby crawl around the living room for an hour. I wish women were encouraged to listen more to their own instincts rather than being told they need a set of rules to follow for every situation. Maybe we can start a new philosophy called *Common Freaking Sense!* Or CFS.

Just don't look for a class near you.